Dedication

To my great-grandchildren

"Piece together what has gone before
To understand
The people who once walked these halls.
For in the home my grandmother created
I find the beginnings
Of the love I have inherited."

From an anonymous poem entitled "Inheritance"

Yes, and then...

Nearly a century ago
Sally grasped a handhold
Onto the incomprehensible wheel that is life itself,
She swung up and on,
As onto a moving trolley,
Bound for she didn't know where
And as she moved,
She found that if she answered, " Yes"
To many of life's questions,
The world opened rich with possibilities

Forward

"Pepper for the Soup"

"I have some pepper for the soup," Sally's voice chuckled to me from my answering machine. "We'll talk Saturday." I smiled at this promise of new recollections from the extraordinary life of my friend, the gifted storyteller and connoisseur of both fine food and original expressions. When Saturday arrived, I asked, "So Sally, first tell me about the origin of the expression, 'Pepper for the soup.'"

Del Sisson and Sally Snyder

"Oh yes" she said. " Well, that came to me quite a few years ago when I was writing an article for a home decorating magazine. I was explaining the ratio of colors that, put together, make the ambiance of a wonderfully satisfying room. There's the **primary color**, the **secondary color** and the **accent color**. And then comes the all-important secret ingredient, the element of surprise that adds zest to the room, *the pepper in the soup.*"

Over my year of Saturday conversations with Sally Meyer Beightol Snyder, I came to realize that these ratios also mirrored the wonderfully satisfying composition of her own life. **The primary color is her family and friends. The secondary color is her professional pursuits. The accent color is the diverse activities she's undertaken purely for their challenge and joy. And then the *pepper in the soup,* the totally unexpected events and people that have popped unannounced into her life.**

The first time I met Sally, she and her husband Dick Snyder were sliding in next to us on a bench in the Standish, Michigan courthouse. We had all come to hear a case that would impact us as property owners. We nodded a quick, silent greeting as the bailiff summoned the court to order. Sally's eyes scanned the courtroom and then came back to rest on mine with a conspiratorial grin and raise of the eyebrows that said, "Isn't this interesting. But we're all in this together. And whatever the outcome, it's not the end of the world, right?" I nodded my agreement, though I realized not a single word had passed between us. I was yet to hear the warm, confident, empowering voice that would decorate the years ahead for me with insights, laughter, lore and wisdom, all drawn from the elements of Sally's intense and remarkable life.

Decades later, January of 2021 arrived with the Covid-19 pandemic raging on in its tenth month. Hoping to elude the virus until a vaccine could be devised, Sally was confining herself in Denver, Colorado, and I was doing the same in Charleston, South Carolina, leaving us both more time than usual at our disposal. Ever the spark plug for activity, Sally discovered a program online that would allow us to play bridge with our bridge loving friends around the country.

I was musing over an anecdote Sally had just shared with us when it occurred to me that this pandemic could actually provide a great opportunity. It could allow Sally and me uninterrupted time to sit down together so that I could capture on paper the narrative that only she knows, the one that weaves together the astonishing, heart wrenching, inspiring, and entertaining events and characters that have peppered her life.

When I called to ask what she thought of such an enterprise, she replied instantly, "Well, yes. Sure! Wouldn't that be great? When should we start?" So, on the 16th of January 2021, with Sally sitting at her phone and me perched at my keyboard 1,700 miles away, we began the dialogues that have given rise to this book.

Del Sisson

Table Of Contents

1965... Sally Finds Her Way into Business

1982... Ups and Down – Downs and Ups

1996... A Dear Old Friend and a New Beginning

2018... Each New Now

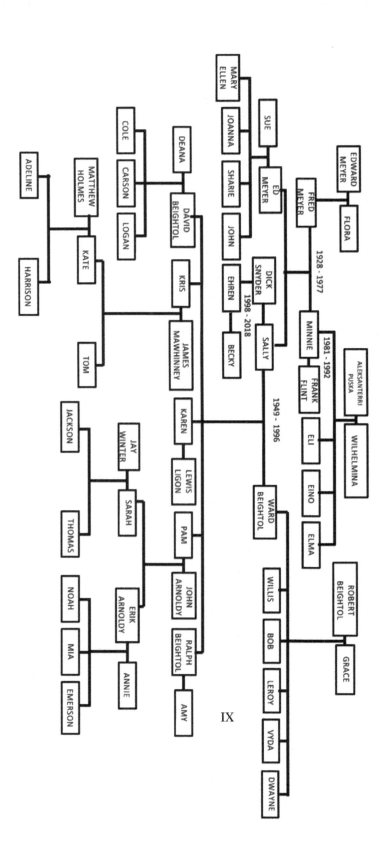

IX

1905...
Minnie

1 - A Rugged Start

"My story really can't begin with me," Sally decided. "It has to begin with my mother's complicated story…"

Sally's mother was born in December of 1905 in a snow covered farmhouse in the tip of Michigan's Upper Peninsula. Her parents named her after her mother, and the family called the little girl Minnie. She was their fourth child.

Minnie's parents, Wilhelmina and Aleksanteri Puska, had joined the great exodus of Finns from their homeland in the late nineteenth century. Finland had fallen under the domination of Russia, its powerful neighbor to the east, who increasingly enforced repressive policies on the Finnish citizens.

At the same time, recruiters from America's timber and mining companies traveled Finland in search of workers. They spoke of the wealth of opportunities and promise to be found in America where there were areas so like Finland.

The Puskas and many of their relatives, made their individual decisions to pull up roots in the farming region of Lahia, Finland and undertake the sea and cross-country journey to begin their lives anew in northern Michigan nearly 5,000 miles away.

The region where they settled i was a mecca for Finnish families. Its landscape, climate and livelihoods looked and felt like home. In this new place, Minnie's father's name was Americanized to Alex Jacob.

The young couple cleared land and established a fine farm. They tilled its soil, planted it with seed, and harvested its crops as they raised their sons, Eli and Eino, their daughter Elma and now baby Minnie.

But when Minnie was only a year old, tragedy struck when Minnie's father was killed in an accident, leaving her mother, who was 26, alone with four young children and the farm to run..

Wilhelmina was married again that same year to a man named Michela Torkka *whose name was Americanized to Mike Norvac*. In marrying the widow, he became joint owner of the farm with the responsibility for its operation, thus enabling Minnie's mother to hold the family together and maintain for them all a hopeful future.

Minnie's mother,
Wilhelmina Puska

The next year, Wilhelmina again became pregnant and gave birth to a daughter, Emma. And then when Minnie was three, an even greater tragedy befell them all. Both Wilhelmina and the baby died, leaving the second husband the sole owner of the farm, which he kept. But he didn't keep the children.

Before Minnie was five, she and her siblings had lost their father, their mother, their home, and then their contact with each other. The three older siblings were taken by relatives.

Wilhelmina's older sister Susanna and her husband took Eino and continued west to the state of Washington. There the boy was given his uncle's last name, Simila. The surname change frustrated Minnie's efforts to locate him when she grew up. After Eino's death many years later, Minnie was delivered a small inheritance from his estate. His gesture touched Minnie deeply but left her longing to have been able to

3

look into her brother's face, understand what he knew of their family, and listen to the story of his life.

Eli was adopted by a relative who moved with him south to the Detroit area where the boy grew up. Sally knows that Minnie and Eli were eventually able to reunite because when Sally was very young, she remembers being introduced to Eli. He was dressed in a Navy uniform and, pointing to the sky, taught her the Finnish word for airplane.

Elma, Minnie's sister, was taken by yet another relative who moved with her to Youngstown, Ohio where she grew up in a secure, comfortable home.

And that left little Minnie. A couple, Mary and Leonard Erva who lived in the area, adopted the child. What their motivation was in adopting the youngster can only be surmised, but the reality was so devastating that Minnie would not be able to speak of it until her own daughter, Sally, was in high school. And then she could never speak of those years without tears.

After Minnie had been given her meager share of her family's possessions: one pillowcase, three spoons and a few items amounting to no more than twenty in all – Minnie was taken away to live in the Erva household. Mrs. Erva directed the bereft little orphan to a back room with nothing but a thin blanket and a bale of straw for a bed. The child was made to clean and polish spittoons to earn her keep, and if she didn't perform to Mrs. Erva's standards, she was beaten. When Minnie was old enough to go to school, Mrs. Erva did not allow her to attend. And when Minnie was entering adolescence, one of the woman's sons and then another went to Minnie's room intent on seducing her, but the desperate girl fought them off.

At last when she was thirteen, a stroke of good fortune came into Minnie's grim life. It was the day the Erva woman sent her to work at the Kempainen farm.

The Kempainens were, again according to research done by Sally's niece Joanna, a Finnish family related in some way to the Puskas.

The large family needed help with the household chores because Mrs. Kempainen suffered from arthritis that confined her to a chair most of the time. But despite her infirmity, Mrs. Kempainen was proactive and positive in guiding Minnie in the tasks she needed to have done.

Minnie quickly fell in love with the whole, kind, fair, hardworking family. Everyone worked, even the little ones, but rather than scrubbing spittoons, the little ones in the Kempainen family were responsible for keeping the flies off the cows during the milking. The boys attended school in installments when they could be spared from work on the farm.

When Christmas came, Minnie's eyes saw under the Kempainen's tree a package with her name on it. Overjoyed, when she unwrapped she discovered a dress that Mrs. Kempainen had made for her. When Minnie carried her wonderful present home, Mrs. Erva snatched it from her and refused to give it back, telling her later that she'd torn it up and thrown it out in the snow.

When Mr. Kempainen, a man of few words, realized the abuse the child was forced to endure, he took his rifle and went to confront the Erva woman.

As the story goes, he issued her an ultimatum and at some point shot over her head to emphasize his seriousness.

She released her claim on the child, and Minnie was welcomed into the fold of the Kempainen family. Sally notes with pride that the Kempainen children grew up to be outstanding adults, one a mentor to Sally's own children. For three years, Minnie lived and worked as one of them. Each night, she told Sally, she prepared a whole peck of potatoes to feed the family.

When Mrs. Kempainen could spare Minnie, the girl was able to attend school. But beginning school in her teens meant trying to piece together years of fundamental understanding she'd missed. She worked to learn and compensate for what she didn't know, but so much felt beyond her reach. When asked many years later what she would have wanted to be if she had had the opportunity, she answered, "an archaeologist." Though she never achieved that ambition, she did bloom as a bright, compassionate, highly capable and stylish woman with a wonderful sense of humor.

Because the Kempainens were a family of boys, Mrs. Kempainen introduced Minnie to a cousin, Esther Puska. The two girls immediately bonded. Soon they dreamed of going to the great metropolis of Detroit to the south where opportunities awaited. They vowed that as soon as they could earn enough money, they would buy train tickets, leave the north and make the 560-mile trip south to Detroit. When at last the day came, Minnie packed her meager possessions and bid a heartfelt farewell to the Kempainens and her early life.

2 - 560 Miles South

When they arrived in Detroit, Esther scoured the Help Wanted Ads and found jobs for herself and Minnie. Esther was hired as a housekeeper for one wealthy family, and Minnie was hired as a companion for the daughter of another. Minnie remained in that position until she was twenty when the daughter married. The family lived elegantly, with gardeners, maids, and chauffeurs, and they saw to it that Minnie had a wardrobe to befit her position as the companion to their daughter. Minnie was 5'3," a pretty, petite brunette. Sally's fiancé, many years later, would later describe Minnie as looking like movie star Hedy Lamarr.

Minnie

Minnie's was a true rags-to-riches story. She accompanied the family on their travels and attracted the admiring attention of young men who were sons of wealthy families.

The son of the Folgers Coffee fortune enjoyed her company as did the son of the Palmer House Hotel fortune, but she was embarrassed by her poor education and felt she would never be able to fit into their lifestyle. She compensated well, but she could not, in fact, read.

When her job as companion to the daughter of the family ended, Minnie was recommended for a position as housekeeper for a Jewish family named the Wagemans. There she learned the secrets of Jewish cooking and acquired a life-long love of lox and bagels.

While Minnie was working for the Wagemans, she and her sister Elma who had grown up in Youngstown, Ohio were at last able to make arrangements to reunite. Their plan was to meet at the train station in Detroit.

Minnie was waiting for the arrival of the train when a woman with a rather grubby looking baby asked Minnie if she wouldn't mind just holding her baby for a few minutes because the woman had something she needed to do. Minnie obliged.

When Elma arrived with a tall young man, Minnie was still holding the baby. The three spoke politely but formally and somewhat awkwardly because Elma and her friend assumed, rather logically, that the baby was Minnie's, and they weren't sure how to address the subject. Finally, when the child's mother returned to claim her baby, the tensions of the first meeting suddenly vanished in spontaneous laughter as Minnie, Elma, and her friend Fred Meyer shared their ready sense of humor.

The sisters looked so much alike, though Elma was blonde and fair-skinned while Minnie had dark hair and skin that tanned easily in the sun.

Sally believes the darker gene may have been carried millennia ago by Turkic people who migrated to what is now Finland. The linguistic similarities in the languages of the Turks, Hungarians and Finns appear to bear this out.

Now Minnie was happily grateful to be a member of a small family of three: herself, her sister Elma, and their cousin Esther.

1923...
Fred

3 - Fred Meyer of Ann Arbor

A year after Minnie, Elma. and Fred Meyer met in the train station, Minnie was working at the Wagemans when she answered a knock at the door. To her astonishment, there stood Fred Meyer, 6'3" and handsome, again smiling down at her. During the intervening year, Elma and Fred had gone their separate ways, but Fred had retained his pleasant memory of Minnie and decided to see her again. Minnie would adamantly insist that she never disrupted a romance between her sister and the man who became Minnie's husband.

Fred Meyer was the only child of Edward and Flora Tessmer Meyer.

Their families had emigrated from Germany to the U.S. through Ellis Island during the last half of the 19th century. Both the Meyer and Tessmer families settled in the area around the university community of Ann Arbor in the rolling hills of southeast Michigan.

The Tessmers purchased fertile acreage outside the city where he planned to establish himself as "a gentleman farmer." He and his wife had three daughters, Flora, Mary, and Rose. Flora's sisters married farmers who owned adjacent farms on Scio Church Road outside of Ann Arbor. And Flora married Fredrich Meyer who owned the Meyer Hardware Store in downtown Ann Arbor.

Height ran in the Tessmer family. Fred's grandfather on his mother's side towered over everyone at 6'4", and his daughter Flora, Fred's mother, was herself "nearly six feet tall with auburn hair and blue eyes – "a real beauty," as her granddaughter Sally described her.

One of Sally's very early memories is of visiting her great grandparents at the Tessmer farm. She sat under a tree eating "neffles" (noodles in brown butter) that Grandma Flora's mother, a small woman, brought to her along with an apple from a tree in the yard. Flora's father, who seemed like a giant to Sally, sat not far away in a rocker on the porch, and Sally remembers being astonished when he took a wooden match and struck it against a well-worn spot on his chair to light his pipe.

Edward and Flora Meyer

Young Fred on the porch on Willow Street

Flora and Edward had married around the turn of the century and built a handsome, gray, stucco house with white trim in Ann Arbor on Willow Street. There they were rearing their son Fred. A large porch ran the length of the front with pillars that rested on a three-foot wall and held up the roof. Willow was a short street adjacent to West Park that had only five houses on each side. The Meyer house was in the middle and set on three lots. In the rear were narrow garages as well as a house for the dog. All along the back of the property ran a deep yard with room for a garden as well as peach, pear and cherry trees, a 20' X 20' raspberry patch and clusters of rhubarb. Flora was a great cook who preserved the bounty growing in the backyard so the family could eat from it all winter.

In 1923 young Fred was seventeen years old and attending Ann Arbor High School. One evening a friend of his father had been visiting at the Meyer house and had had too much to drink. Fred's dad was worried when his friend stubbornly insisted on driving home, so Fred's dad got in the car with him to be sure his friend got home safely. Fred's mom followed behind in their car. But the friend's car veered off the road and into an electrical pole. When Fred's father got out to inspect the damage, he didn't see the live, disconnected, electrical wire lying on the ground. He stepped onto it and was instantly electrocuted.

In that instant, young Fred Meyer's life changed. His parents had planned that when the boy's schooling was finished and he was well-prepared, he would take over the family business. But now everything was changed. The grieving young son was suddenly required to leave high school and assume responsibility for operating the store and supporting his mother and himself.

As Fred struggled to acquire the many new skills now expected of him, he was grateful, and would always be, for the young man named Nip Schneider who ran a metal shop at the back of the hardware store. Nip and Fred dove easily into a friendship that lasted their entire lives. They shared the same passions for sports, the out-of-doors, mechanics and eventually powerboat racing. Nip was a resourceful and welcome support as Fred struggled to keep the store operating successfully.

By 1927 when Fred Meyer knocked on Minnie Puska's door, he was 21 with four years of experience running the store under his belt. The euphoria of the 20s still held sway: Prohibition hadn't begun; the stock market hadn't crashed; the Great Depression hadn't arrived; and the first shots of World War II hadn't been fired. It felt like the right time for these two, young, hardworking adults who had known such grief to make a life of their own together.

Minnie   Fred

1929…
And Now Sally

4 - A New Young Family in the Neighborhood

Willow Street home today

Fred had begun courting Minnie at about the same time that Art Clark, a fireman with the Ann Arbor Fire Department, was courting Fred's mothe, Flora. When Flora and Art married, they made their home just a few miles away from Willow Street. So when Minnie and Fred married on July 28, 1928, the Willow Street house was their home. It was the first true home that Minnie had ever known, the place she and Fred would call home for nearly half a century.

Around the same time, Nip Schneider, Fred's best friend, fell in love with and married Esther. They made their home not far from Fred and Minnie, and Esther and Minnie also became lifelong best friends. Minnie and Esther shared the everyday joys and concerns of maintaining marriages and households, and they loved to play bridge.

It was to the Willow Street home on April 28th, 1929 that Fred and Minnie brought their newborn Sally. Grandma Flora's doctor had delivered her at his private hospital in Ann Arbor.

5 - Growing Up On Willow Street

Growing up on Willow Street, Sally thrived under the strong, loving, female tutelage of her mother and her grandmother. The diminutive Minnie and the impressively tall Flora laughed and collaborated easily together. With her mother-in-law, Minnie learned the secrets of great German cooking to add to her already considerable proficiency in Finnish and Jewish fare.

Sally remembers with delight that her Grandma Flora drove a little electric car when Sally was very young. It was like a buggy without a horse that she steered with a push handle. Flora would drive it to church and on errands. She was a shopper and happily took her little granddaughter along with her on her outings. Sally remembers her grandmother picking her up and seating her on the glass counter at the Bertha Muhlig Dry Goods Store so everyone could admire her. She was treated like a princess.

Grandma Flora treasured the wonderful, old, German, Christmas traditions her family had carried with them to America, and she took delight in sharing them with her family. There

Sally with her lollipop

were large and delicately made ornaments of glass and beads and frosted wire that caught the light. A spot in the large, high-ceilinged, front hall on Willow Street was perfect for a full tree that reached to the ceiling.

In the German tradition, Christmas trees were not put up until after children were in bed on Christmas Eve. From her first Christmas on, Sally was enraptured by the wonder and breathtaking magic of the magnificently bedecked and lighted tree on Christmas morning. Christmas trees would remain a fascination she shared with her own children and a source of particular joy her entire life.

Minnie took pleasure and pride in this bright little daughter of hers, and having Sally allowed Minnie to engage in childhood experiences she had been denied. In first grade Sally was learning to read and was excited to share with her mother the skills and techniques she was acquiring. Minnie eagerly gathered them in and applied them, learning to read right along with her daughter. Minnie became an efficient reader, though she never really mastered the finer points of writing. She naturally had a head for numbers but rarely wrote them down.

Minnie and Sally enjoyed endless games of jacks, and they loved cooking together. When Minnie decided it was time for them to learn to sew, Sally read the pattern, and her mom followed the directions as the two made a dress for Sally. Pleased with the progress they were making, Minnie had Sally put the dress on. "Sally Ann, put your arms down," her mother said.

"I can't," Sally frowned as Minnie helped her out of the dress. They went back to the pattern instructions and found they had missed the step, "clip the curve." Without
clipping the fabric where it curves at the armhole, it was indeed impossible for Sally to put her arms at her sides." So together they problem-solved and taught themselves the fundamentals of sewing, a skill Sally would apply her whole life and teach her own children as well.

Her mom sometimes took Sally with her to the beauty shop. One day when the women at the shop asked Sally what her daddy was doing, Sally answered honestly that he was "home making beer." This drew both smiles and raised eyebrow since
it was during Prohibition.

In 1936 when Sally was seven, her brother Ed was born. Sally found having a baby brother an interesting new activity, and she appreciated him as a built-in playmate when he grew older. He was fun to be with and like Sally, gathered friends easily. Sally would often make the half-hour walk by herself to visit Grandma Flora,

Sally and baby Ed in 1936

16

especially when Art was "working a shift." Sally remembers being with Grandma Flora in the bathroom and washing her face with soap and water. Her grandmother reached over and gave her a smack on the bottom. "Sally Ann, never wash your face with soap! Promise me you will never do that again." And Sally didn't. Grandma Flora's other beauty secret was using cocoa butter to ward off wrinkles. Whether a regimen of no soap and cocoa butter caused their skin to be smooth, or it was the result of their good genes, neither ever developed wrinkles.

Grandma Flora also had a passion for orange sherbet. Sally remembers the two of them walking down the hill to the store together where they would buy a pint of the sweet cold treat to enjoy as soon as they got back home to play cards. Grandma Flora loved playing cards and happily made Sally her protégé. They started with "Go Fish" and rummy and loved playing double solitaire. Sally says the two "had decks of cards in our hands all the time."

Minnie enrolled Sally in tap dance and piano lessons. Sally loved the wonderful sound of her taps as she danced to "The Sidewalks of New York." – "East side, west side, all around the town…" The Meyer home had a piano, and Sally practiced her way through the Third Piano Book. So it was her job to play "Jingle Bells" on the piano each Christmas morning to announce that the great, long-awaited day was "Right Now!"

Her parents and the Schneiders would have been up late into the night decorating the tree and arranging the gifts Santa had left. The year there was a Lionel train for Ed, his dad and Nip had so much fun playing with it and testing out the little pellets that made the locomotive emit smoke that for a time it seemed to be broken, even before Ed had laid eyes on it.

When the Montmorency cherries were ripe in the Meyer backyard, Minnie, Sally and Ed would climb up into the trees to pick them. There were invariably more than they could use, so Sally and Ed were allowed to take their wagon and go around the neighborhood selling baskets of cherries. There was great demand for them, and the kids did very well.

Sally and little brother
Ed

6 - Threshing Time

Each summer while she was growing up, Sally couldn't wait for threshing time. Grandma Flora's sisters, Rose and Mary, had married men who owned adjacent farms. Rose wed Henry Klager and Mary wed Louie Schwartz. After the wheat had been harvested and left to dry in the fields, Grandma Flora, Minnie and Sally would drive to the Klager farm at 3110 Scio Church Road.

Since all the wheat of an area would become dried enough for threshing at about the same time, the farmers from the surrounding

Klager farm at threshing time

farms would engage equipment and pool their muscle and resources to rotate from farm to farm threshing the wheat to separate the edible kernels from the stalks. Everywhere, Sally recalled, there were wagons and horses. Working as a team, the farmers could complete a whole farm in one day.

It was at Aunt Rose's farm that the women from the farms around would gather to feed the threshers. A table would be set up in Rosie's house that ran through the parlor, the dining room and into the kitchen. Sally remembers the happy, purposeful bustle of the women as they prepared enormous bowls and platters of food for the ravenously hungry men when they came in from the fields. Out in the yard Sally would watch as one man would pump water as the next washed off the chaff and dirt before they stomped off their work boots on the porch and came in through the screen door to take seats at the long table. Every kind of meat, side dish, pie and dessert would be served at lunch as well as dinnertime. Sally loved it! But the very most fun of all for Sally was being allowed to "swim in the grain" as it showered down into the silo. The kernels were dry, slippery, and pleasantly cool - perfect for swimming. In retrospect, it was probably very dangerous, Sally says, but no one knew, and it felt like heaven.

10 year old Sally

7 - Parenthood

When Fred lost the hardware store during the Depression, he focused his energy on finding work. He took it wherever he found it and managed to stay employed throughout the years of the Depression when so many others were without jobs. Then he was hired to work in a grocery warehouse, and this was the beginning of what would turn into a career in the groceries business. As he demonstrated his competence in the warehouse, he was recognized and promoted. He first worked for the Berdan Company and then for Lee & Cady. IGA, the Independent Grocers Association, was just getting underway when Fred joined them. Its mission was to make it possible for small independent grocers to compete in a market increasingly dominated by the big chains such as A&P and Kroger. Fred was sent out on the road to assist grocers in the layout of their stores and to see that the many stores in the IGA network in Michigan and Ohio were supplied properly.

When he worked, Fred always wore starched, bleached, long-sleeved, white, cotton shirts. The Meyers owned a "mangle," an ironing device with heated rollers. Minnie taught Sally to use the mangle, and Sally took pride in her skill. She could iron one of her dad's big shirts in six minutes.

The responsibilities of maintaining the house during the week while Sally's dad was away could be demanding. The family relied on a coal furnace in the basement to keep the house warm in the winter. When coal was ordered, it was delivered by a truck with a chute that sent it rumbling down into the Meyer's coal bin in the basement. During the week, it was Minnie's responsibility to shovel the coal from the coal bin into the furnace as needed throughout the day. Too much coal at one time could ruin the draft and smother the fire. Too little might allow it to burn out. It was also important to be mindful of "coal gas," a toxic vapor that furnaces could emit and cause an explosion if not correctly ventilated. At night the fire had to be properly "banked" to last until morning. And periodically the fire needed to be allowed to burn all the way out so that the accumulated cinders and ash could be shoveled out and removed.

When the weather was cold in the winter, the first floor register that was closest to the furnace (the metal grate over the duct from the furnace) was everyone's favorite place to be. The air above the burning coal in the furnace billowed up and expanded, its welcome warmth dissipating as it reached the registers in the further reaches of the house. But there just above the furnace, the lush extravagance of warmth was indescribably wonderful.

Minnie discovered that the ledge just inside the door of the furnace was the ideal place to bake beans. She would prepare them and then allow them to bake all day long until they reached perfection.

Fred would return on Fridays. So Minnie always committed Fridays to cleaning and preparing so that everything was calm, clean and beautiful when her husband got home. Sally and Eddy were responsible for chores and for being sure not to disturb the perfection.

Many years later Sally's own children would question why they could never do anything but clean at home after school on Fridays when all their friends were already enjoying their weekends. She realized that she had automatically replicated her mother's practice and that perhaps it didn't fit Sally's own quite different family.

Minnie found work too in a ball bearing plant, looking very much like Rosie the Riveter. She hired a woman to take care of the kids and cook while she was working, but the woman was such a terrible cook that Fred insisted Minnie quit her job after 3 months so the family could eat well again.

Her dad worked hard, was successful, and provided well for the family. Whenever he was free, he indulged his passion for sports. He and

Nip loved the testosterone-laden euphoria of powerboat racing on Whitmore Lake in their single-person, bullet-shaped boats that went slap slap slap as they roared down the lake and across the finish line. Esther and Minnie took their kids and enthusiastically cheered on the racers.

Sally says her dad was "quite an athlete." He made "All American" in the Volleyball Association Championships for adult men. Each summer he participated in Ann Arbor's summer YMCA volleyball camps where he acquired many good friends. He reveled in the sportsmanship and the camaraderie he felt with them

Sally also remembers that her father made no effort to disguise his racial animosity. Sally's mother, however, would stand up to him and insist that he hush. Only once does Sally ever remember real tension in her parents' marriage. She was so small her feet didn't touch the floor. Her mother cried and cried, and that made Sally cry. Behind closed doors Sally could hear raised voices. Sally assumes now that there must have been a dalliance by her dad, and she remembers that her mother spoke of "leaving," but somehow they overcame the crisis, and to Sally's great relief put it forever behind them. Sally had no doubt that her father adored her mother

Sally remembers that her mother got a parakeet that she named Cookie whose cage was in the dining room. Minnie worked diligently to train the little bird to talk, repeating over and over, "Cookie is a rascal," and sure enough, the bird learned to talk but never to pronounce the letter r. Cookie would announce what sounded exactly like, "Cookie is an asshole." To silence the bird's embarrassing profanity when polite company was around, Minnie would throw a cover over the cage.

8 - The Elementary School Years

West Park After the Snowfall

      Sally's Willow Street neighborhood teemed with kids who piled out of their houses to play marbles, tag, red rover and jump rope. In the Bennetts' yard was a mulberry tree shaped like an umbrella that you could sneak under to "tell lies." After dinner, the kids went out to play hide and seek all over the neighborhood until the streetlights came on.

      Just down the hill was West Park. It was in a large basin that had the look, Sally said, of something a giant might have scooped out. It had athletic fields, a band shell where concerts and events regularly took place. It had swings, slides, seesaws and a jungle Jim, but Sally and her friends loved most of all chasing through the "Indian trails" that threaded the hilly slopes around the park where they would create marvelous, swashbuckling adventures. The football field was flooded in the winter for skating. Near it was a little "warming house" where skaters could go to thaw out. To this day, Sally can close her eyes and summon up its smell - of wet woolen mittens steaming as they dried by the stove.

She was a natural athlete like her dad and in the winter loved playing crack the whip with the boys, especially when she got to be the one at the end of the whip holding on by one hand as she flew over the ice. She loved tobogganing on the hills with her friend Dick Snyder. When her brother Ed got big enough, he joined them too. Minnie would send Rip, their big, sweet, smart, brindled, Doberman/boxer mix to the park when it was time for the kids to come home for dinner. "Go get the kids," Minnie would say. The three of them, puffing clouds of breath into the waning evening sunlight, would ascend the hill and the front porch. Sally and Eddy, cheeks, nose and toes still crimson, would peel off their snowy boots and leggings in the vestibule to race for the glorious warmth of the central register in the main hall to thaw out while Minnie put the wonderful smelling dinner on the table.

Though Dick Snyder and Sally Meyer were in the same grade, they went to different elementary schools, living on opposite sides of West Park. She went to Mack, and he to Tappan.

At Mack, Sally was in Mrs. Gowdy's sixth grade class. Sally remembers the times Mrs. Gowdy would put her hand on Sally's shoulder - probably Sally had been daydreaming – and recite for her a passage from poet Charles Kingsley's *Youth A Farewell:*

My fairest child, I have no song to give you;
No lark could pipe to skies so dull and gray;
Yet, ere we part, one lesson I can leave you
  For every day.

Be good, sweet maid, and let who will be clever;
Do noble things, not dream them, all day long
And so make life, death , and that vast forever
  One grand, sweet song.

Sally would retain the words of the poem as well as Mrs. Gowdy's mandate charging her to a life of doing, not merely dreaming.

When Sally wasn't daydreaming, she was very busy. Some weeks she took part in youth activities at Trinity Lutheran, her family's church, every day of the week. She belonged to Girl Guides, very much

Swimming at camp

like Girl Scouts, and sometimes she earned money babysitting.

She spent two, happy, engaged weeks each summer at the YMCA camp, Camp Tacoma. She loved it all – swimming, horseback riding, fishing, crafts and the friends she made. She said it never occurred to her to be homesick.

Also during the summers, Sally's family, along with their friends the Schneiders and Bennetts, rented a large cottage together at Pontiac Lake near Ann Arbor.

These were happy social times. Sally remembers that the drink of the adults was "Old MacNish and well water." Each year the families would create a movie. Sally laughs at the recollection of her dad, beer bottle in hand and wrapped in a blanket with lipstick markings on his face, in his role as the Indian chief. Every person had a role, and there was always a papoose.

The Schneiders, Meyers and other friends, the Bennetts, decided to purchase a large swath of land in Montmorency County where they could all enjoy roughing it. They called it their camp. En route, Sally recalls, they always stopped about half way up at Iva's in Sterling for a chicken dinner.

Then they would stop again to buy the most delicious, fresh, home-baked bread from a woman on a farm before the last leg to their camp.

Camp included a crude tarpaper-covered cabin, an outhouse and a sauna. There was a big iron cook stove that sat 25 feet away as a precaution to keep the cabin cooler in the summer and safer

Iva's Chicken Dinners

from the risk of a house fire. Sally remembers picking blueberries that grew there in such abundance and making a deep-dish pie. Then they fed wood into the stove all day as it baked. And it was delicious!

To brighten the interior of the cabin, Sally's mother whitewashed it. Whenever they left, everything had to be packed away in sturdy barrels to avoid rodents. Minnie was very particular about what went where and would be frustrated to find things just tossed in every which way after the men had been there hunting and fishing. Isolated as it was, the cabin was broken into regularly, so nothing of value was kept there. Sally's dad dug up fir saplings and a cherry tree from the property that he transplanted to their home in Ann Arbor. The saplings flourished in their new environment and grew rapidly, the firs to tower high above the house.

9 - Visiting Minnie's Sister Elma in Ohio

Every summer until Sally was in high school, Minnie took her to spend two weeks with Minnie's sister Elma and her family in Youngstown. At the same time, her dad took her brother to spend time at their camp in Montmorency County in northern Michigan.

In Youngstown, Elma's childhood had been so unlike Minnie's. She had been adopted into a secure and caring family with the means to take care of her. Elma fell in love with Don Lewis, and they married and had three sons: Bucky, Jimmy and Duke. Sally was very fond of her cousins, and they spent endless happy hours together playing baseball.

The Lewis family lived on the top floor of a Victorian mansion with a huge porch and winding staircase to the second floor. Elma was a beautician, and she and Don were in business together. On the first floor of the mansion was their large beauty shop that had 20 or more operators. Don was especially pleased that the business had contracts with the town's funeral parlors. Don saw to the grooming of the recently deceased in advance of their funerals.

Minnie was always amazed at the unstructured nature of mealtimes at the Lewis house. Perhaps 25 boxes of cereal would be laid out for breakfast. In the center of the table was always a 14" bowl filled with coins of all denominations, probably tips from the salon. The kids, including Sally, were expected and encouraged to take a handful of coins to go to Isley's to buy themselves lunch and perhaps an ice cream cone whenever they chose to. If they had change, they could just put it back in the bowl. Nobody kept track. And in the kitchen was a big electrified roaster that would be filled every morning with whatever they would eat for dinner.

Don was outgoing, interested and interesting. He ran for mayor. If one of his sons took a course, Don would take it too. Don loved engaging in dialogues that were held each week when ministers from all religions in town got together. She remembers the story of Uncle Don asking the Baptists who believed in full immersion what they did with the sacred baptismal water afterward. Did they just let it go down the drain?   Years later, Sally's husband Ward would love talking with Uncle Don. Sometimes their philosophical conversations would last all night. Elma and Don's sons all became successful adults: one a minister, one an electrician and one a plastics engineer for the Samsonite Company.

Don and Elma's eldest son Bucky, the Samsonite engineer, would years later invite his mother and his Aunt Minnie to accompany him on a business trip to Finland. Bucky had little familiarity with the Finnish language, and through lack of use, Elma had lost any skill she had once had. To everyone's delight, however, Minnie found that the Finnish language that was so much a part of her childhood came flooding back to her, and she understood everything. The trip was a joy!

Once Elma, Esther and Minnie found each other, they stayed present in each other's lives. When Sally's own children were youngsters, she and her husband bought her Aunt Elma and Uncle Don's well-used Winnebago to take the family camping in the mountains. Minnie and Elma's cousin Esther was able to continue her education and even earned advanced degrees. She become the Registrar of the ILIFF School of Theology in Denver. She found her career enough and did not marry.

10 - The Teenage Years

In Ann Arbor on December 7th, 1942, Sally was thirteen years old and out riding her bicycle when she heard a paperboy shouting, "Extra! Extra! Japan Bombs Pearl Harbor. America at War!! She remembers racing home to tell her parents. The war would be the backdrop for Sally's life for the next years, but she paid as little attention to it as possible. At the same time, the young man in Webster City Iowa who would become her husband six years later was preparing to go to war.

But in Ann Arbor young Sally Meyer and Dick Snyder attended Slauson Junior High together where they were in Mr. VanElls' homeroom. Mr. VanElls taught science and quickly recognized Dick's interest in science and his steady competence. He hired Dick to help him make slides and find worms.

Sally and Dick's seats were close to each other, and they continued the happy, easy friendship they'd established at West Park. With their class they rotated to teachers in other rooms for Latin and Algebra and such and then returned to their homeroom for study hall.

One day an assembly was scheduled, and Mr. VanElls' homeroom was making its way to the gym. Dick maneuvered himself to a place beside Sally and then reached down and took her hand. It was the first time a boy had held her hand, she said with a laugh, and she was "all twitterpated." She had only recently begun to menstruate and wasn't accustomed to the new changes in her body.

For Sally, junior high was a time of expanding new social experiences. Dick and Sally were part of a group of friends who hung out together but didn't specifically date. In the summer they would meet at the band shell for Thursday night concerts, and in winter they tobogganed at West Park.

When Dick was fourteen he got his driver's license. With Nuel Smock and a couple of other friends, he drove to Sally's house to pick her up. They were reveling in their new freedom and belting out the Sunday school hymn, "Yes, Jesus Loves Me." And Sally says, "It's a good thing He did!" because someone opened a passenger-side door

Sally Meyer and Dick Snyder in junior high
yearbook

right into Dick's lane of traffic, and Dick knocked the door off. Sally was petrified! What would happen? What would they do? What would this mean? But Dick calmly stepped out and took charge, appearing not at all phased. He made the necessary arrangements, and life went on without complication. Sally was impressed at the poise and character her friend demonstrated. His parents clearly also trusted his competence because they allowed him to take the car for a week of camping and fishing with his younger brother, Jack, when he was fifteen and his brother thirteen. Sally, however, did not learn to drive until she was in her twenties. Her dad told her that his car was their livelihood and that its safety had to be their highest priority. "You can drive my car when you can afford to buy one," he told her.

Dick not only liked Sally, he liked her mother, and she enjoyed him. Interestingly, though, Sally never actually met Dick's mother. The reason could have been Sally's light blue, angora sweater.
On Friday nights, Dick would get the car and pick up their friends to go to the dance at the YMCA. On the Friday night Sally wore her sweater, it looked great, but it also shed onto anything that came in contact with it. So when Mrs. Snyder's son came home with blue angora on his suit coat, his mother was outraged. Even though Dick explained that they were honestly "only dancing," she retained her doubts. "Don't ever dance with that girl again!" she told Dick. But it would be over fifty years before Dick told Sally what his mother said because he thought it would embarrass Sally. It just " wouldn't be right."

Sally in high school 1947

The long, comfortable, appreciative friendship of two kids who were exactly the same age – their birthdays just a week apart - continued. It was Dick who gave Sally her very first kiss. And it's quite likely that the mutually appreciative relationship between Dick and Sally would have continued to develop on through high school and perhaps beyond, but for one thing: Sally got tall, and Dick didn't. She became a 5'9" statuesque 36" 26" 36," while Dick remained his junior high height for several more years. So in high school they gradually drifted in different directions, and as Sally says, "lost each other."

She dated guys in high school who were tall. And since Ann Arbor was a university town, she also drew the attention of college guys with more experience than she had. Her father advised her that relationships worked better when couples were about the same age and matured together, but Sally was having fun and enjoying the flattering attention she was drawing. She remembers getting to know the young Gordie Howe before he became the great Red Wings Hockey star and Bill Fleming before he became the noted University of Michigan sportscaster.

Hogan and Hayes Furriers

The first job Sally had in high school didn't pay very much, but it was impressive. She and several other girls were hired to model fur coats in the windows of Hogan and Hayes Furriers on South Main. The shop was located on a corner with showcase windows that wrapped around two sides. The challenging part for Sally was that it was necessary for the models to wear high-heeled shoes, something, being tall, she had never had on her feet. She and her mom went shopping and found shoes that fit just fine, but walking in them was another story altogether. She wobbled and tottered. Ever becoming able to walk with grace and ease in heels looked like a challenge she could never meet. Her mother would insist, "Sally Ann, put the shoes on and keep practicing!" "Oh I hate it," Sally would groan as she put the shoes on and did as her mother said. Finally, finally she got the hang of it. And what did the girls wear under the coats? Hogan and Hayes had them wear bathing suits.

Sally got another job as a model at the Boat Show where she sat smiling in that same bathing suit as she now adorned Chris Craft boats. Then at Christmas time she worked as a sales clerk. And when as a senior she'd finished her high school graduation credits by the middle of the year, she took a job in a lab at the Health Department until her commencement exercises in June. In the lab she worked alone, cleaning petri dishes and doing other not very interesting tasks. She noticed there a huge pad of official birth certificates that were used by the Health Department to record the birth of a new baby. Each day that pad sat there, and each day Sally thought how cool it would be if she and a few friends had birth certificates that would "prove" they were of legal age. She finally gave in and tore six sheets from the huge pad. Feeling both guilty and exhilarated, she exited the lab with the certificates and carefully typed one and a spare for herself and kept the others for special friends she would select.

Sally recalls her senior class planning a trip to the beach. The class president was a smart, well-loved young black man named Walt Sellers. When they all arrived at the beach with their bathing suits and picnic paraphernalia, they were told that Walt wouldn't be allowed to swim. No matter their efforts to persuade the park manager, he would not permit it. The students were shocked at the blatant racism. She wished she could say that they all stood with Walt to confront the injustice, but they didn't. The White kids swam, and exactly what Walt did, she didn't know. It was 1947.

All of Ann Arbor's high school students were given a test during their senior year that determined whether they qualified for scholarships to the University of Michigan. Sally had not been a particularly focused student in high school; as she says, she was "unconscious." So both she and her family were surprised when Sally qualified for a full scholarship. At seventeen, though, she had accepted a small engagement ring from a medical student at the University of Michigan who smoked a pipe. His parents lived in Ann Arbor and had already ordered a house from the Sears and Roebucks catalogue for the young couple. Sally remembers trying to quietly make her way into the house and upstairs to her bedroom and hearing her father's voice from the dark first floor bedroom saying, "You know nothing good happens after midnight."

11 - Not So Fast, Sally

Sally's dad did his best to redirect his high-spirited daughter. He made the decision that she would not accept the scholarship and insisted, instead, that she "go away to school." She was accepted at Michigan State that at the time was still a college, not yet a university.

Wells Hall

Sparty, Michigan State mascot

Her parents paid her tuition and drove her with her clothes and her sewing machine to Wells Dormitory in East Lansing where she met her new roommate, Pam Wood.

Sally received a $4.00 a month allowance from home, and she worked in the dining room when breakfast was served. She wore her little engagement ring and stayed in while everyone else went out. But before too long she decided she didn't really want to be married. Her father knew she was not going to be able to resist the opportunity to have fun.

Sally hadn't a plan as to what she should study. She would discover only much later that her interest and talent actually lay in business, but that hadn't yet occurred to her. She did know, however, that her dad was involved in sports and they interested her too. She decided to become a Recreation major with the thought of working in YWCA administration. For two years she studied fencing, golf, hockey and baseball.

On campus there were a lot of WW II veterans in their 20s taking advantage of FDR's GI bill which paid tuition and a stipend for living expenses to those who had served.

Sally had been dating Arnie Anderson, a young vet who lived in an apartment with three fellow vets not far from the campus.

One day he and his roommates were bemoaning what poor cooks they all were when Sally chirped in that she would cook dinner for them sometimes if they knew what they wanted and bought the ingredients. She was not a great cook, she laughs, but she'd learned more than they had by spending time with her mother and grandmother in the kitchen. She could definitely roast a turkey or make a pot roast. She says she found it gratifying to cook for "such hungry and grateful guys."

Sally and Arnie
Anderson

1948...
Michigan State and
Ward Beightol

12 - Their "Radar Was Up"

Arnie invited another of his military friends, Ward Beightol, over for dinner the night Sally was cooking. Arnie and Ward were both Air Force pilots who had flown rescue missions in Gooney Birds during the war and had become good friends in Paris when they'd been stationed there. So what a shock and wonderful surprise it had been for them to run into each other on the Michigan State campus. Arnie, Ward and Ward's brother Willis were interested in making use of the GI Bill. They had all been drawn to Michigan State in particular because of its comprehensive testing policy that could facilitate earlier graduation for vets who were eager to be on with their careers. The policy said that if a student passed the first term of a full year course, the student could test over the content for the entire year. If the student passed that test, credit could be granted for the entire year.

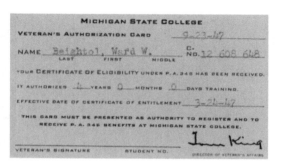

Ward's GI Bill veteran's authorization card

Ward and Sally met over the dinner she had cooked for Arnie and his roommates. Ward was a tall, handsome, self-assured fellow with black hair and black eyes. It was quickly clear that he was extremely bright with an inventive mind. He'd first enrolled in the School of Engineering, but others advised him that engineers were currently a dime a dozen and that he should transfer into Psychology, which he did.

Ward was nearly seven years older than Sally, but there was an electricity between them that Sally felt and was quite sure he did too. "Our radar was up," she said. When she got back to the dorm that night she told Pam about this fellow she'd met. Pam asked what he looked like. Sally replied, "I have no idea, but his voice is amazing. Oh, and he has such a great smile, and the way he winked." She put his name on her bulletin board – Ward Beightol - and expected an imminent call. So she was surprised and disappointed when it didn't come day after day.

Jussi Bjoerling program

Over the next six weeks she occasionally saw him when they ran into each other on campus or when they were at the apartment together with friends. He was always pleasant and charming, but that was as far as it went.

Ward loved music and had a fine singing voice so he was overjoyed to discover that the renowned Swedish tenor, Jussi Bjoerling, would be performing in concert on campus. Thrifty though he was, he bought four tickets in the first row: two for Arnie and Sally and two for himself and his date. At the last minute, Arnie called Sally to say he'd had an invitation to play basketball which sounded better to him than the concert of a tenor, so he asked her if she minded if another friend of theirs, John, went in his place. Sally agreed that that would be fine. But then when John arrived to pick Sally up, they agreed that neither of them really really wanted to go and hear the tenor either. Instead they went to the bar.

In order to be admitted into the dorm late, Sally needed a program that proved she had been engaged in "cultural enrichment" and certainly not just having a good time at the bar. So she and John went to intercept Ward after the concert. He was livid when he saw them. How could they not come when he had footed the bill for such incredible tickets?!! Guiltily they made peace as best they could before Sally asked Ward if she could use his program to get back into the dorm. Still steamed, he reluctantly gave it to her, telling her he wanted it back because he had notes on it. The program got Sally back into the dorm that night, and Sally pinned the program on her bulletin board smiling: "If Ward Beightol wants his program back, he is going to have to come and get it." It spent six weeks on Sally's bulletin board.

Then one day Arnie Anderson called Sally and asked if he could come and talk with her. When he came he asked, "Hey, do you want to get married?"

"What are you talking about?" she laughed.

"Just thought I'd ask," he said. He hadn't thought about it either. Ward had been the reason he had asked. Ward thought Arnie was serious about Sally, and honor would not permit him to jeopardize his friendship with Arnie by flirting with Arnie's girlfriend. When Arnie assured Ward that he and Sally were only friends, Ward wasted no time in calling Sally and asking her out, but Sally wasn't free the night he had in mind. She suggested an alternate day. He hesitated just a bit before saying that the graduating party for his class was to be held that night......but.... of course, he would love for them to go out that night instead.

Ward in civilian dress

The attraction they had been holding in check for what felt like an eternity was at last free. They were crazy about each other and quickly head over heels in love. It wasn't long before Ward called to take her to a particularly nice restaurant for dinner. Sally was surprised because Ward was frugal with his money since he had so little of it. They ordered steaks, but Ward could scarcely eat, and Sally ended up finishing his meal as well. Then he nervously got to the point. Would she marry him? She was thrilled. "Well, sure," she said. But the idea of getting married right away wasn't as appealing to Sally as it was to Ward. In retrospect she thinks she was too young to get married, but she has no regrets. He was nearly seven years older, had traveled, had experienced great danger and real loss and was fully ready to settle down. She had two more years before getting her degree and was enjoying her life as a coed. She suggested with a grin, "Why don't we just fool around and then get married?" He grinned back with a wink, "No. Let's get married and then fool around." That was April, and soon they had wedding plans for August.

Sally continued living with Pam in the dorm and completing her courses until spring term ended. Ward lived with his brother Willis and his wife Jean in a nice off- campus house and worked on his Master's degree. Ward and Sally babysat Willis and Jean's kids in exchange for use of their car. One of the little tykes they babysat, Ward David, would years later become a pilot and work at high levels of Special Forces Intelligence.

Ward met Frank Johnston in an advanced math course they were both taking. Frank asked Ward if he played bridge and if he might be interested in joining him in a tournament. Ward answered yes to both questions. The tournament, it turned out, was the State Tournament, and the two won!!

Ward loved to play bridge and wanted Sally to enjoy bridge too. So Sally played her first game of bridge with Willis, Jean and Ward. Though Ward was a gifted player, he was not a gifted teacher. Ward explained to her that sometimes it's wise to "duck" a trick, which means not take it when you can because you have a strategy in mind. Sally found she was very good at ducking, though the whole strategy part was still a mystery. It was years before Sally realized in an "Ah Ha!" moment that bridge was actually a game of numbers. Then the game's mysteries began to unravel for her.

13 - The Beightols of Webster City, Iowa

Ward went home to Webster City for a brief visit to to assist his mom. Webster City was a small, forward-looking city of about 7,000 in north central Iowa. It would produce two Pulitzer Prize winners in 1956 and 58, and hometown boy Dan Akroyd would take tickets at the local theater to promote the opening of his new film, Blues Brothers years later in 1980.

Grace Townsend Beightol

Since Ward was eager to introduce his fiancé to those back home, he asked Sally to join him. She flew to Des Moines where Ward met her, and

Bud Hovland

they had lunch with his longtime childhood friend, Bud Hovland. Bud was then working as a disc jockey at radio station WHO in Des Moines. A talented vocalist as well as an irrepressible tease, he told Sally that Ward was such a sweetheart of a guy that he would have married him himself if he were not a guy.

Eager to prove herself a worthy daughter-in-law-to-be, Sally stepped up to help Ward's mother, Grace Townsend Beightol, by hanging the laundry to dry on the clothesline in the yard. Sally was taken aback by the look of horror on the face of Ward's mother when she came into the yard to see that Sally was hanging Mrs. Beightol's bloomer-type underwear out in clear sight, rather that putting the garments in a pillow case. Sally quickly apologized when she comprehended her faux pas, though she had never heard of such a practice.

Ward's mom was about 5'6," a sturdy, fair-haired, plump woman with a big bosom. Though Grace wasn't highly educated, she taught herself whatever she needed to know. She loved poetry and taught herself to play the piano.

The family had moved to Webster City from Fort Dodge where the four oldest children - Vyda, Dwayne, Willis and Ward - were born. Willis was delighted when he had been allowed to choose Ward's middle name, Weldon. And from the beginning, Willis had taken his little brother Ward under his wing. Ward's earliest recollections involved Willis in Fort Dodge. He recalled that Willis had climbed up a ladder into a tree, and little Ward was doing his best to follow him up. Willis insisted he go back down because it was too dangerous for him. Ward also remembered the time Willis was chopping with an ax and cautioned Ward to move out of the way so he wouldn't get hurt. Ward did move but only moved to stand behind his brother. When Willis swung the ax back, he hit Ward in the head and was devastated to realize he had hurt this little brother he was so committed to safeguarding.

In Webster City, Grace's husband owned a successful Ford car dealership, and the family had a lovely home with a sunroom, a music room, hot and cold running hard and soft water, and a beautiful garden. Everyone came to the Beightol house for Sunday dinner. In Webster City they had their fifth child, another son, Leroy.

Then when Grace was pregnant with their sixth child, her husband Bob died of a hereditary heart condition. In short order, Grace was widowed, the economy collapsed as the Great Depression set in, and the dealership and their lovely home were lost.

Vyda and Dwayne, who were teenagers when their father died, had spent more of their lives as privileged children than had their younger brothers. They experienced the abrupt change in their lifestyle with sharper awareness. Vyda married Elmer early as the Depression was taking hold, and Dwayne joined the Navy. Grace was left with no alternative but to figure out how the rest of the family would survive and then take charge to see that they did.

She found a modest house to rent from a man known to the family as Mr. Sorensen. It had enough acreage for a large garden - 150' to the railroad tracks and 50 feet wide. She rallied the boys to help with the garden as soon as they were capable, and the family relied on the food from the garden for their survival.

Young Grace

Willis was in elementary school when their father died, and he rather naturally assumed the responsible role of father figure for the younger kids in the family. Grace decided that though Ward was only four, he was bright and ready for school and would be able to handle it. She explained to Willis that he must take Ward with him to school. Whatever explanation Willis gave at school, Ward was allowed to remain.

There was so much to grieve, but Grace hadn't time to grieve. Heavily pregnant, she was struggling to sustain and stabilize life for her family while also managing two tots at home as well as her demanding mother. Her mother was a strict, impatient Methodist who believed playing cards was sinful and took every opportunity to preach to the boys and often chased them with a broom.

Grace would make knickers for the boys out of used suit pants from the Goodwill. Ward said he never had a pair of long pants until he bought them for himself when he was in high school. Each year Mr. Sorensen, their landlord, would gift the family with one warm, fleece-lined, waterproof, oilcloth coat. So each year the eldest received the new coat and initiated the handing down of each of the previous year's coats to the next in line.

As the boys were able, they took on the responsibility for maintaining the garden and kept it "perfectly." Grace carefully canned what the garden produced, and it sustained them year around. Nearly all the meat they had was what the boys hunted. She would give them each three bullets and instruct them that they needed to come home with some game. She canned the ducks, squirrels, pheasants and jackrabbits they killed. She filled shelves in the basement with tomatoes, corn, beans and other produce from her garden. She put up applesauce, peaches and other fruit that she was able to obtain in bulk or trade for as she did for eggs and milk. From the ceiling she hung onions, and potatoes she kept in a bin. Grace bought as little as she possibly could - only sugar, flour,

Ward, Leroy, Willis, Bob and Dwayne

salt, oatmeal, and occasionally bacon and the great indulgence, a jar of sorghum that the boys adored on pancakes and on anything else they could sweeten with it. Grace saved the bacon grease, and the kids loved it on pancakes with brown sugar. They were never hungry. She also bought for them cod liver oil, which they all detested.

Grace and the boys created a small stand where she sold sloppy joes, earning a modest income. She also sold Traverse Bay Woolen Mills blankets door to door. As the kids got older, each was designated to be financially responsible for one of the family expenses. Ward was responsible for paying the telephone bill. He earned money by delivering papers, so in the winter he made boots for himself by slicing old tires and strapping them onto his feet. In high school he earned money by dashing between the two movie theaters in Webster City and running their movie projectors. He had to coordinate the sports that he played with the timing of his movie job. Years later he designed an automatic rewinding system that would allow the film to rewind as the movie was being shown. Ward's fertile mind was always hatching inventions and clever adaptations, but to Sally's regret, he invariably moved on before patenting or marketing his concepts.

The children learned the virtues of frugality and resourcefulness from their mother. They teased, that she would "walk a mile to save a nickel." Grace took advantage of everything that was free. On Wednesdays, admission was not charged at the community swimming pool because it was the day the pool was cleaned. So the family swam every

Wednesday, and Grace would bring a picnic. Only on the rarest of occasions would the boys be able to get their very favorite treat of all – a hotdog! At Christmas they trekked to the woods to cut down their

Christmas tree and haul it home to decorate with popcorn and cranberries.

The Beightol boys were all bright, inventive, experimental problem solvers. Their lives were far from grim, and they also found time to get into mischief. Ward and his friend Bud Hovland were

Ward, Leroy and Bob

fascinated with airplanes and decided to build one of their own. They pilfered a rolled up awning to make the skin of their plane. No one suspected them of having anything to do with the missing awning until the identifiable pattern on the awning bled through the paint they had used to cover their plane. They were nabbed and required to repay the owner of the awning the cost of a new awning.

Grace took the boys to church and Sunday school where they learned all the hymns. They loved music and they loved blending their voices. Ward would later become a devoted "barber shopper." The family loved storytelling and poetry. Ward said their mother "would make the big boys cry" with the poems she read. And Grace was a reservoir of maxims and expressions that Sally deftly taps to this day:

"Chicken one day - feathers the next."

"You can't judge the depth of the well by the length of the handle on the pump."

"Never send a boy to do a man's job."

"If I never see the back of my neck…"

Grace also occasionally found reason to employ one rather off-color one that Sally chose not to acquire: "Love goes where it's sent, even if it's under a dog's tail."

Ever Ward's mentor, Willis advised his brother when he was in high school to save up $5.00 and put in an application to the community college. Ward followed his advice and after high school earned a number of credits, some in French, before pivoting to follow Willis's example and enlisting in the Air Force in July of 1943 when he was 21.

By the time Ward had qualified for his wings and was at the award ceremony to receive them, who but Willis, by then a colonel, flew in with great pomp and flourish to personally pin the wings on his

The young flyer

younger brother. "It was a BIG deal!"

Willis was a skilled, experienced, and decorated pilot who flew in the daring and dangerous Ploesti Oil Field Raids to deprive the Nazis of their voluminous oil supplies in Romania.

e Daily Freeman-Journal

dvance; Italian Mutiny

Colonel Beightol in Raid Over Rome

Ward too became an exceptional pilot who flew gasoline to General Patton at the front and flew rescue missions, often in the mountains behind enemy lines.

The brothers all served in the military and became successful in their own fields.

Dwayne Beightol, Leroy Beightol, and Bob Beightol

When Dwayne returned from his service in the Navy, he created a printing business in Webster City. Unfortunately he also periodically suffered from PTSD and slept in the vault of a bank, because it was where he felt safe.

Leroy's patent

Leroy invented a self-hardening cast that he patented. Johnson and Johnson bought the rights for it in order to keep it from competing with their own product.

And Bob became a computer whiz and created an organizational system adopted by Mutual of Omaha.

After Grace's children were all out of the nest, she and Mr. Sorenson married. This was the same Mr. Sorensen who'd gifted the boys with warm oilcloth coats and who had rented to Grace the house in which Grace had raised her boys. They enjoyed the next years together, taking opportunities to fish, an activity they both deeply enjoyed.

By the time Ward and Sally flew back to East Lansing, the amazing characters, setting and story of Ward's family were playing like a Broadway musical in her mind.

14 - A Wedding in August

When the term at Michigan State ended, Ward borrowed Willis's Chevy to drive his fiancé back to Ann Arbor. When Sally was alone with her dad, she asked his opinion of her fiancé. He replied somewhat grudgingly, "At least he's a man this time, and the ring's a little bigger." Fathers don't easily relinquish their daughters.

Sally recalls with a chuckle taking Ward to introduce him to her grandmother and Art at their cottage at North Lake not far from Ann Arbor. Grandma Flora and Art were entertaining friends, and Grandma Flora was having a great time shooting craps on her knees on the floor with the guys. Sally hadn't known her grandmother to shoot craps before, but when she looked at Ward, she saw he was grinning.

Sally and her Grandma Flora

Then there were so many wedding decisions they needed to make! The wedding would be held at the family's nice, intimate, old church, Trinity Lutheran. The reception would be at the house on Willow Street since there were three "giant rooms" across the front of the house. In the middle room would be the wedding cake, and the food and beverages in the other two rooms. The wedding presents would go into the bedroom. They would whitewash the basement and cover the workbench in white paper since the keg and the dancing would be there. This was to be "a good, old-fashioned, German wedding."

Sally remembers that Ed was eleven at the time and was exploring the gifts Sally and Ward had received at a shower. One was a silent butler, which is a little container with a handle, and a hinged top that is used for collecting table crumbs or ashes from ashtrays. Ed examined it and said with a wry grin, "And look. It's big enough for two."

Minnie decided that before the wedding the bathroom, the house's only bathroom, a large one on the second floor, needed to be painted a cheerful yellow, and Ward got to work on the task. Sally popped in to see how Ward was coming along with the project, and in the process Sally looked down to again admire how handsome her new engagement ring looked on her finger. To her alarm, the diamond had turned yellow! "Oh, no! Oh, no!" she cried in horror until Ward assured her there was nothing wrong - the diamond was merely reflecting the yellow of the bathroom. Ward needed to get back to East Lansing for his classes, and he also needed to return Willis his car. So Sally and Ward bid their anguished farewells.

As students, neither of them had saved money, so Sally set about finding a job in a dress shop for the summer. And Sally and her mother got busy with the planning. They needed to decide about the food, the cake, and the flowers. As for the dress – this was something on which her parents were willing to splurge. They went to a special dress shop in Ohio her dad had learned of and found the perfect dress. Its price tag was nearly $200.00, an extravagant amount in 1949, but it was exquisite. In fact, both her daughters Kris and Pam would wear it years later when they married.

The trip to Ohio for the dress was marred by a scare when Minnie who was about 40 began suffering unbearable pain. They made it home and took her to the University Hospital in Ann Arbor where it was discovered that she had a tubal pregnancy that required immediate surgery. To everyone's relief, she recovered after several days in the hospital.

Then they were back at their wedding plans. There were the invitations and the guest list. In addition to Sally's friends, there were Esther and Elma and Don and their boys on her mother's side. Then there were the Meyer family

Sally in her perfect bridal gown

51

and friends including her dad's volleyball team and their wives. There was Frank Johnston, Ward's bridge partner, and his brothers Willis and LeRoy and his military buddies. Ward's mother originally said she would attend. She would fly in the private plane of Ward's friend, Bud Hovland, who was going to sing in the wedding. At the last minute, however, a decision was made that Leroy would attend, and since there wasn't room for two passengers, Grace stayed at home. As it turned out, Grace never attended any of her sons' weddings.

When the great day arrived, August 6, 1949, about 100 guests poured into Trinity Lutheran Church on Williams Street. Her roommate Pam was Sally's maid of honor and Willis was Ward's best man. Sally looked heartbreakingly beautiful in her perfect gown. Bud Hovland sang, "Yours is My Heart Alone" with such full-throated intensity that when he reached for a pareticlar note, the bowtie at his throat popped off. The memory of that moment would bring chuckles to the guest for years to come. The food, the cake, the dancing, and celebrating went on and on until Sally's dad was found asleep on the bed amongst all the wedding gifts.

It was a terrific wedding, and Sally Ann Meyer was now Sally Ann Meyer Beightol. Reality set in more quickly than anyone would have hoped the next day. Ward needed to address a call he had gotten from his mother shortly before the wedding explaining that his brother Dwayne's print shop had the contract to print the telephone books for all of Webster City and environs, and that Dwayne was in terrible condition and couldn't get the orders out as promised. She was sorry to ask him, but would Ward be able to come home very soon and help? Ward had arranged for a secluded honeymoon for himself and his bride at a fishing camp. But his mother's request was compounded by the fact that the stress and perpetual motion of the months leading up to the wedding had caught up with Sally, and by the next morning she had a fever, cough and sore throat that turned into pneumonia. The only thing that made sense was to postpone their honeymoon and for Ward to go to expedite the printing of the phone books. The groom went to Iowa, while the bride stayed home to get well.

15 - Newlyweds

Ward and Sally made their first home in a cute little apartment in Lansing by the railroad tracks at 737 1/2 East Shiawassee. Everything shook "just like in the movies" when the trains went by. The landlords were Hedder and Spurgeon Hubbell who were from Kentucky or Tennessee and lived on the first floor. Sally laughs, "Ward would be playing Rachmaninov while the neighbors would be playing, "Does Your Chewing Gun Lose Its Flavor on the Bedpost Overnight?" An outside stairway led to Sally and Ward's apartment on the second floor, and the house next door had the same arrangement, so Sally and Ward could look in the window of their neighbors and catch portions of TV shows as they ascended and descended.

Ward was simultaneously pursuing his Master's degree in Psychology and working in a program for the deaf and blind. Sally was working in a dress shop in Lansing, and money was tight. They had gotten a car, but it was a gas-guzzler, and affording gas for the tank was an ongoing challenge. When Ward would get to the top of the long steady grade that led to the dress shop, he would turn off the ignition and coast all the way to the shop without using any gas. Sally would visit the grocery store every day to find the most inexpensive and nutritious foods available. After the first meal Sally cooked, Ward asked her, ""Weren't there peas left from yesterday?" Sally had to admit that she had thrown them out. His frugal mother had instilled in her kids that you never waste anything. And Sally learned to make soup from any meat or vegetable that wasn't eaten.

It was while they lived in their

Mr. and Mrs. Ward Beightol

Lansing apartment that Sally discovered she was pregnant and where they first brought their little David home. He was born April 21st, 1950, a week shy of Sally's 21st birthday. He had black hair and black eyes like his father

Hedder and Spurgeon were always friendly and ready with advice or a folk remedy. They advised Sally who had bloody noses during her pregnancy to put a dime on the roof of her mouth to stop them. And then when David was born advised that if he developed colic, to put 2 drops of kerosene in the baby's bottle.

They had been in the apartment about a year and had lovingly painted and redecorated it when the Hubbells decided to raise their rent, perhaps figuring it was only right for their tenants to pay more for the privilege of living in such an improved space. By this time Ward had completed his coursework, was working on his thesis, and had taken a job in Mason, Michigan working for the State of Michigan counseling jailed kids and additionally helping write laws for the juvenile court system. Unfortunately while Ward was at work one day, a disturbed young man impulsively hurled a peck of potatoes that hit Ward without any warning. It resulted in an injury to Ward's back that would bother him his entire life, but as Ward always did, he pressed on.

It was a sensible time for the Beightols to move to Mason which was a town about 15 miles closer to work for Ward than where they were in Lansing. They found a charming renovated barn to make their home and purchased a wonderful, white, shag, 9'X12' rug that they adored. It was lush with nearly three-inch-long shag, but they found it had a major deficiency that allowed its price to be affordable- it could not be vacuumed. Shaking it clean was a monumental challenge! But their life together seemed to be shaping up in a rather orderly and enjoyable way.

When their little David would wake in the night to feed, Sally would wake Ward up so they could admire and play with their amazing baby before everyone went back to sleep.

And Fred and Minnie were enchanted with this magical new extension of their lineages. Amongst it all, Ward focused on his thesis whenever he could.

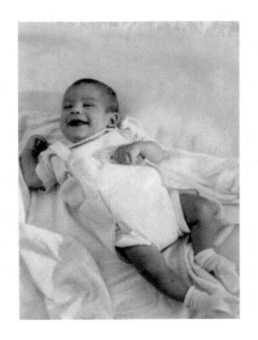

Baby David

1952...
Ward is Recalled to Active Duty

16 - So You've Got a Plan

Once Sally, the fun-loving adventuress, accepted Ward's proposal of marriage, her life began changing in ways she couldn't quite imagine. A new life had grown within her body and then slept in the circle of her arms. So she and Ward crafted new roles for themselves as parents. They sketched out plans for their future and made the executive decision that they would be a family with two children – " lovely and appropriate." So they planned the birth of their second child to take place about 2 years later, good spacing for their "lovely and appropriate family."

Then changes began happening that Sally not only couldn't imagine, but that she had no control over. When they'd been in Mason about a year and Sally was pregnant again as planned, suddenly Ward was notified that he was being recalled to active duty because of the threat posed by Communist aggression in Korea. He was being ordered to Colorado Springs, Colorado.

Sally, Ward and David on Kiowa

They packed up David, their plans, their wedding gifts, and what furnishings they had accrued. The military transported their possessions to Colorado Springs while the Beightols drove. They found a small house on Kiowa Street in a residential area of Colorado Springs and settled in.

But shortly after they'd gotten settled, they were sent to Montgomery, Alabama where Ward was to take nine weeks of training in Aviation Medicine. So they headed back east-southeast to Montgomery where they moved into a little, furnished, guesthouse behind a much larger main house. It was their first experience in southern living, and they were horrified at their first encounter with what Sally described as "flying cockroaches" that were 5 or 6 inches long and that sounded like noisy drones when they were in flight!

While Ward spent each day in school learning, among other random skills, about how to deliver a baby, Sally was at home with the very busy David. She washed his diapers on a washboard in the bathtub, and one afternoon when she was distracted for a moment, David disappeared. She called his name, searching everywhere and was beginning to panic when she looked up the road, and there was a Black lady with David in tow, bringing him home from the direction of the big house.

Sometimes it all felt a bit surreal, especially when a chorus of deafening cat yowling announced some competitive mating ritual was underway beneath their porch. When Ward got home and heard the clamorous racket, he somehow came up with a firecracker that he lit, and the amorous felines went scrambling. And then after nine weeks Ward graduated first in his class.

17 - Figuring it Out

Colorado Springs

The little family headed back to Colorado Springs and the house they had left at 810 Kiowa.

Ward reported to the base as Sally got resettled and prepared for the arrival of their new baby.

Kristy made her appearance that summer at Fort Carson - July 6th, 1952. Sally and Ward were delighted. Now their family was complete as planned, one boy and one girl. However Ward was astonished that this newborn was blonde, blue-eyed, and fair-haired - such a stark contrast to David and Ward's coloring. Ward actually double-checked to be sure there had not been a mix up in the nursery. He was assured that the only other child born that night was the child of a Black couple, so the towheaded Kristy was indeed their own. Sally reminded Ward of the time the two of them were walking and saw a cute little blonde baby. Sally had said that she'd like "one of those." Ward laughed, "See? You and your wishes!" Kristy would grow up to be the spitting image of a Beightol. Sally noted that she looked and walked just like her dad.

In Europe during the war, Ward had flown rescue missions in the mountains in workhorse, propeller-driven planes called Gooney Birds. In Colorado as part of the 8th Air Rescue Squadron, he again flew Gooney Birds, but these were retrofitted with jet engines. The squadron was charged with the dangerous mission of flying under the radar in the US so the US government could determine how to anticipate enemy challenges if they occurred. They "came in low and got out fast," Ward said.

When someone in Colorado Springs questioned Ward about the danger inherent in flying in mountainous areas when he had small children at home, he replied,

Gooney Birds

"Oh, with each new child, I fly a thousand feet higher."

Ward was sent for survival training to the mountains during the winter. Among the meager supplies they were each allotted was pemmican, a nutritious dried paste made of melted fat, dried meat and berries that could be kept for up to five years without any refrigeration.

Ward and the Air Rescue Squadron

It was a staple in the Native American diet, but the others in his training group were not at all fans of it. At the end of the training, they were happy to give all that was left to Ward, and Ward was delighted to take it. He brought it home to Sally, and she made great chili and spaghetti out of it for months.

Ward would regularly be away on duty for five days and then would return for two or three before leaving again. Though he was devoted to Sally and their family, he was also devoted to his responsibility in protecting the country. Sally says that of the first eight years they were married, he was gone 50% of the time. So 24/7, Sally's constant companions were her children. And still feeling very much like a kid herself, she found great joy in simply playing with them as her mother had done with her. She decided that she and her children would all somehow just "grow up together."

Nevertheless, with Ward gone, Sally was the lone individual charged with executing decisions and meeting responsibilities. Fortunately she had strong women as role models who didn't buckle in the face of challenges- her grandmother Wilhelmina, her Grandma Flora, her mother and Ward's mother. But still, especially when she was ironing, a shiver might wash over her accompanied by a vision of a figure in uniform walking up to the front porch and knocking at her door and telling her Ward was dead. Since her mother was a great believer in premonitions, the dread was harder to shake off.

Their house sat at the rear of a lot behind a larger house and was isolated enough along one side and the back to make it an accessible target for an intruder. Once an intruder broke in and stole all of Sally's underwear. Another time, either the same person or someone else wrapped the curtain around the vacuum cleaner and stole wine from the basement that Ward had stored there. On yet another night the babies were asleep in their cribs, and Sally was asleep in her bed when she heard David saying, "Someone at door." Sally instantly thought of the gun she kept that had been in her family, but she realized she didn't know how to use it. Instantly she called the police and paced with her heart in her throat until she heard the sirens. The officers investigated and found the would-be intruder had moved a trashcan to be able to climb on it and had removed the window screen to enter. The officers cautioned her to "be careful" and said they were astonished that her husband would allow her to be there alone by herself with two little kids.

This could have been the point at which many young women might have resented and resisted the changes being imposed on them, but Sally simply didn't. She says she guessed she was too busy trying to make everything work. Since the family had no choice but to make do with whatever time was left for them to be together after the military had taken its share of Ward's time, Sally needed to figure out creative solutions to perplexing riddles. She put busy little David on "clothesline duty" on a tether so that he could be safe outside in the yard while she dealt with the baby and the house inside. She would call, "I see you!" as he'd peek back over his shoulder as he again tried to push the limits.

Ward loved the idea of playing golf on the weekends, but that would mean he was gone even more of the time. Sally decided that if she took golf lessons during the week, she could learn to play so they could play together on the weekends. But the golf pro insistently "hit on" her until she asked Ward to forego the golf and instead be with the family. And he did. Though she couldn't control events, she could control how she responded to them.

It was in Colorado Springs that Sally practically and rather symbolically decided to get her hair cut. Until then she had braided it and worn it tucked around the crown of her head. But if she wanted the use of the car while Ward was away, which she definitely did, she had to be up, have breakfast fixed and have the kids organized when Ward's copilot came to pick him up. She could do all of that, but she couldn't also brush, braid and wrap her hair. If she wanted the car, the hair would have to go. Short hair allowed Sally and her children greater access to the world beyond 810 Kiowa.

Sally with wrapped braid

18 - Not Reno?

Orders came down that the Air Rescue Squadron was being relocated from Colorado Springs to Reno, Nevada, 1100 miles west. Ward made arrangements for a suitable house for the family in Reno. The movers came and packed their furniture and belongings which were to be unloaded at their new house in Reno in a few days, as soon as the

Off to Reno

house was available. Sally in the meantime packed what the family would need for the week or so until they could be settled in their new place. Their plan was to stay with friends, the Ogles, in Reno until word came that they could move in.

But after perhaps a day in Reno and before Sally even got to see the house, Ward received an abrupt change of orders. He was not to be in Reno; he was being sent to Africa. He had been selected because of his skill and experience as a command pilot as well as his fluency in French to be the personal pilot and interpreter for General Hutchinson who worked in strategic American operations in Rabat, Morocco. Ward and a crew would fly the general whenever and wherever he needed to go.

Sally asked Ward how, having grown up in Iowa, he'd become so fluent in French. He said, he had studied French in school, but most, he added with a smile, he had learned "on the pillow." That was during his bachelor days in his mid 20s when he was stationed in Paris after the Normandy invasion had at last started to turn the tide of the war. With the bruised city at last liberated from the Nazis, hope began to breathe there again. Ward continued to fly missions because the war was far from over. After his missions he returned to Paris glad to be alive and eager to engage with, not merely observe, the Parisian life that pulsed all around him. So he readily made use of the French he had learned in school. He loved the city's cafes, music, clubs and people, especially the

Ward in Paris with his French companion

girls. He even had a casual friendship with Edith Piaf, the great café singer who made "La Vie En Rose" such a sensation. He learned the vernacular and became adept at the off-hand use of slang. And he steadily expanded his vocabulary as he acquired a perception that was uniquely French. When he was finally discharged back to the US in 1947, the French fluency he had refined returned with him. Now in 1953 he was going to Morocco to put his French fluency to use again in a country that had been occupied by the French for many decades.

Ward was notified that if he intended to bring his family to Morocco, the Moroccan government required that he pay rent six months in advance. Ward made arrangements to rent a house in Morocco, and in the meantime, the military movers took everything that had been on its way to their new house in Reno, everything including the perishables they would have been using imminently, and shipped it all to Morocco.

Ward put into the car what things Sally had packed for the family to tide them over until their house was ready in Reno, and with them they set off across the country to Ann Arbor. Sally and the kids would stay with her parents until it was time for their departure for Morocco. Minnie and Fred were a bit awestruck by the changes in their daughter's life, but they were also delighted to have the opportunity to be with their grandchildren until the time came.

Ward kissed them all goodbye and headed back across the country with their car, which would also be loaded onto the ship with their other belongings for the voyage to Morocco.

In Ann Arbor, Sally and her mother shopped for the items that were needed to augment what little Sally had packed, and they kept an eye out for what they thought would be helpful in Morocco. Sally signed up for French lessons since Morocco was a French speaking country. But she got the Spanish she had learned in high school mixed up with the French she was trying to learn. The result was a curious jumble.

Kristy with Grandma Minnie

Kristy with Grandpa Fred

When the phone rang at 909 Willow Street some weeks after her arrival, it was Ward on a noisy, military, trans-Atlantic, phone connection from Morocco. She was so glad to hear his voice. Then came her news, "Honey," she said, "I'm pregnant."

"You can't be," he said with a shocked laugh. They were being so careful about their birth control.

"Oh, yes I am," she confirmed. It had been too early when he had left for her to realize it. "This is crazy!" they both agreed.

So by the time she and the kids hugged her parents goodbye at the train station in Ann Arbor, she was 23 years old and six months pregnant with their third child.

The kids found the train exciting and distracting, and they hardly touched their French toast in the dining car, what with all the whooshing and clicking, rattling and shifting. Their train car had double bunk beds, but the kids were accustomed to cribs with secure sides and couldn't settle down, so no one really slept.

When they disembarked from the train in New York, Sally had eight bags and a stroller as well as David and Kristy with her little chenille security blanket. Sally discovered she had mistakenly gotten off too early and needed to find a cab that would take her on to Grand Central Station.

Grand Central Station

The city was "dripping hot," and though she had snacks for the kids, they hadn't really eaten. The cab took them under the station, and they found the military bus they were to board. The bus sat idling, spewing fumes out into the muggy air as military mothers and their children prepared to board. When it was Sally's turn, she and the kids stepped up and into an unbelievable din. Every child on the bus was screaming, and every mother looked as though she wanted to. Sally quickly remembered the string of suckers her mother had packed "just in case." She rummaged until she found them and walked up the aisle passing them out to the kids. At last the horrendous noise abated and everyone took a deep breath.

The driver maneuvered the bus up and out of the station and headed toward Fort Hamilton where Sally and the children would stay the three days before the ship departed for Morocco. The bus driver apologized that there would be no help for the passengers in managing their bags and their children at the fort. As a result, they would have to manage by themselves.

So Sally stood at the curb in the drizzle with a stroller, two kids, a big belly, eight bags and no help. How was she to do this??? She took a deep breath, put Kristy in the stroller, took one bag and asked David to hold onto the stroller as they made their way to the dorm where they would stay. The room, blessedly, had two cribs. She lifted the kids each into a crib and played peekaboo with them as she backed toward the door, slipping out of sight and popping back into view, with longer and longer time lapses in between each "Peek-a-boo!" while they watched with anticipation for when she would pop in again. When she was finally able to slip out the door, she turned and made a dash back to the curb for two more bags, ignoring the sign that said, "Do not leave your children unattended at any time." She would then race back with the bags and pop back in with a "Peekaboo!" which made the kids laugh. She continued the game until all the bags were in.

Now, what to do about food? Even the milk in the baby's bottle had curdled. She checked the info in the room and found that the mess hall was about a block away. Because there seemed no earthly alternative, she ignored the sign again and left the kids in their cribs and raced with her round belly to the mess hall which she found wasn't serving at the time. But she picked up crackers and milk and a few other things she could carry and raced back to the dorm to her unhappy children. They ate, and finally with full tummies and thoroughly exhausted, finally slept, and Sally lay in her bed and cried.

The next day she discovered there were community showers, which worked well enough for adults, but not for babies. She found a washtub and dragged it and filled it with warm water to bathe the kids. All of the moms with small kids recognized what a godsend the idea was and commandeered a second washtub as well. Life began to make more sense with regular meals, baths and familiar cribs. Sally would tuck her children in with stories and songs, and they would all sleep.

While they were at Fort Hamilton, Sally was summoned for an interview. While she held Kristy, David ran around. The interviewer questioned her about religion and other matters before he asked if in Morocco she could entertain for the general because the general's wife didn't entertain. She was surprised by the request, but being Sally, she didn't have to think long. "Well, sure!" She enjoyed meeting and conversing with people and planning delicious things for them to eat and drink. If those were the qualifications, she had them. She did have to promise that in her role, she would never speak of religion.

She was directed to a doctor's office and given an injection that she was told was required before the eight-day sea voyage to Morocco. Sally thought nothing more about that injection until years later when the baby she was carrying, Karen, was a teenager and needed to undergo a hysterectomy and live her life on hormones. The probable cause was that injection.

Those onboard the USS Geiger were an odd combination. The Geiger was a troop carrier, and most of its passengers were troops who were single or far from their wives or girlfriends. Also onboard were the wives whose husbands were stationed overseas awaiting them. Sally notes, "There was a lot of fooling around." Sally with her big belly was an innocent observer.

U.S.N.S. GEIGER (T-AP 197)

Because of Ward's new position, Sally and the children were not placed in the ship's regular quarters but in the cabin of a Navy captain's wife. At first the captain's wife was a bit standoffish, saying she really had no interest in children. But while she was standing next to Sally and the kids on deck as they passed the Statue of Liberty, the ship sounded its deafening horn, frightening David. He threw up his hands, and she stooped down and picked him up and reassured him. From then on, things were just fine amongst them all. She helped where she could and as much as possible left the cabin to the family, often only returning to sleep. This gave Sally an opportunity to get the kids acclimated to the space and into a consistent schedule. At the beginning of the eight-day trip, Kristy hadn't walked yet. But the floor of the cabin was linoleum and always felt icy cold. Bright little Kristy quickly figured out that she was much more comfortable if only the soles of her shoes were on the floor, rather than her hands, her shins, her knees and her bottom. She stood herself up and walked.

Sally and the kids were even seated at the Geiger captain's table for their meals. And young officers adopted Sally and the kids. They made themselves available to help and entertain them, knowing that, with Sally being pregnant, they wouldn't be accused of having ulterior motives. Sally played shuffleboard and cards with some of the young officers while others carefully tended to and delighted the kids. Sally said she "made out like a bandit."

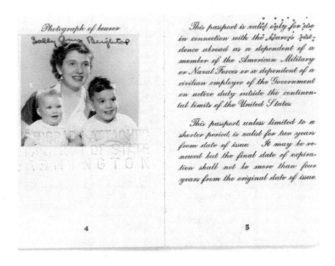

Passport with Kristy and David

19 - Ward at Work - The Cold War

Captain Ward Beightol

What had triggered the escalation of international tensions that caused Ward to be called up was the 1950 invasion by USSR-backed Communist North Korea into Western-backed, Democratic South Korea. Both powers had nuclear weapons, and the tensions of the Cold War that ensued were extremely high.

American strategists felt it was critical for the US to position itself as a powerful deterrent to further Soviet aggression, and Morocco was to be pivotal in this strategy, located as it was in northern Africa. From bases in Morocco, American bombers would be able to penetrate the territory of the Soviet Union and its allies, but Soviet technology did not yet have the capability of retaliating back against Morocco.

The fact that France, an ally of America, controlled Morocco made the arrangement particularly ideal.

Ward's skill set matched perfectly with the American strategy. He was extremely bright, experienced and knowledgable in matters of aviation, **and** he was remarkably fluent in French, allowing him to function as a skilled liaison between the French speakers in Morocco and the Americans. When asked how it was that he had received this assignment, he replied modestly, "Probably they just put in 'pilot who speaks French,' and out came my name."

The military's administrative headquarters were in Rabat where General Hutchinson, Ward, and about 100 officers and fewer enlisted men spent much of their time. A new American Air Force base had just been constructed at Sidi Slimane about 70 miles from Rabat. There the planes of SAC, the Strategic Air Command, were based as well as the plane Ward piloted for the general - the Gooney Bird that had been fitted out for General Hutchinson, though it still had propellers rather than jets.

Ward's work with General Hutchinson, in addition to piloting him on his travels, was frequently in the Interpreter's Bureau. He might be asked to make a speech in French explaining an American perspective on a particular issue. Or he might as an interpreter be asked to tactfully facilitate agreements between the French and American governments.

20 - Morocco

It was just after daybreak when the Geiger entered the port of Casablanca on Morocco's Atlantic coast that summer of 1953 and Sally first glimpsed the exotic setting in which they would make their home for the next two and a half years.

Morocco, about the size of California, has three distinct regions: the moderate coastal plain with its cities and agriculture, the increasingly rugged Atlas Mountains, and beyond them the Sahara Desert. The cultural history of the region stretches back 3,000 years to the Phoenicians and Carthaginians before the Roman conquest and the coming of the Islamic conquerors in the 7th century. Morocco has been a crossroads of cultures for millennia, lying just eight miles from Spain across the Straits of Gibraltar.

On the deck of the Geiger, Sally and the children were seeing who would be the first to spot Ward after their nearly half-year separation. Sally recalls that she could make him out in his uniform leaning against a stone wall. Only Sally, her kids and a handful of other passengers were leaving the ship in Casablanca that morning before the Geiger continued on to other ports.

Ward had driven to pick them up in their own car, the one that had been shipped along with all of their belongings from Colorado Springs. Tucking bags and kids into its familiar interior, they set off to see for the first time the home that awaited them in Rabat an hour away. Rabat was the capital and home to the mysterious Casbah and the great open-air bazaars called souks. The current city was built in the eleventh century on the remains of the westernmost outpost of the ancient Roman

Empire. the great power politics of the nineteenth century, Morocco became a French protectorate in 1917. Rabat's architecture was massive and stunning with elaborate walls, minarets, monasteries, mausoleums and museums reflecting its complex and shifting history.

The house in which they would live at 44 Rue de Chastenae was concealed from the street by an eight-foot stone wall with a wrought iron gate. The wall was coated with brown tadelakt, the durable, lime cement that has been used in Morocco for 2,000 years. The gate opened into a formal courtyard of sand and rock in the midst of which rose a tadelakt coated house with windows that were sixteen feet high. The width of the front door was eight feet with a lock that could only be opened with a golden key as big as an iPhone. The house was built into a slope that allowed a walkout basement in the back where their nursemaid would live. An outside stairway at the back of the house led to a separate apartment where an American family with a young child lived.

The Beightols opened the front door of the house and stepped into a formal entryway as big as a bedroom with polished terrazzo floors. They would be the first occupants of the house. It was fully furnished, and everywhere there were antiques. On the left was a large living room about twenty feet long with a great fireplace. Its tall windows had long gauzy curtains that billowed in the wind.

The dining room

When Sally years later watched the movie "The Great Gatsby" and saw the scene in the room with the billowing

73

curtains, she was struck by how identical it was to the feeling of the living room of their first house in Rabat. A wrought iron railing separated the living room from the equally large dining room that held a massive dining room table. They couldn't believe how astonishing it all was. It seemed that somewhere a decision had been made that if Sally and Ward were going to entertain for the general, they were going to do it in dignified style.

Sally discovered, however, that the kitchen was remarkably small, and the stove with its oven was no wider than a placemat. Sally would find the oven just big enough to roast a turkey if the turkey wasn't too big.

Their belongings from Colorado Springs had been unpacked and placed where they belonged. They settled the kids in that first night, but they did find that the fact they had no screens did not mean there were no mosquitoes. Everyone woke up the next morning covered with itchy mosquito bites. Ward promptly arranged to have the house sprayed which helped immensely, and they learned not to be too surprised when an occasional bird flew in. But at last they were all together.

21 - Fatima, Boaza and Yvonne

Managing her children, her new house, her role as hostess and her new way of life might have been a far greater challenge had it not been for Fatima, Yvonne, and Boaza. Their wages were appropriate in the Moroccan economy but astonishingly reasonable by American standards. Nonetheless, they were pleased to have steady employment. Boaza was a gardener with a gift for making things grow. Yvonne was a nursemaid who cared for the children, and Fatima helped in general with the house, the laundry, the food, and sometimes the kids.

Fatima was 16 years old and her own person. She had a young child cared for by her mother. With no common language, Sally and Fatima over time patched

Fatima with the kids, Karen, David and Kristy

together a means of communicating that wasn't very efficient but more or less worked. Every day Fatima took it upon herself to wash the terrazzo floors.

One day Sally made arrangement with Fatima rather than Yvonne to take care of the kids because Sally had a meeting. The time they clearly agreed for Fatima to arrive was ten o'clock, but ten came and went without any sign of Fatima. The next day Fatima showed up at her regular time. "Why didn't you come yesterday as we agreed?" Sally wanted to know.

"Inshallah," Fatima replied. It was the will of Allah that she'd run into this other person, and what could she do? It was the will of Allah.

Another day Sally was demonstrating for Fatima how to prepare an egg, but Sally accidentally broke the yolk. Afterward, no matter how Sally tried to clarify that breaking the yolk was not what she wanted her to do, Fatima always broke the yolk.

Ward asked Fatima if she knew how to build a fire for their fireplace. Fatima confidently assured him that she did, and he watched as she stacked the kindling and logs with care, but he didn't notice when she got the can of gasoline and poured it on the logs. When he looked back in on her again, she was just striking the match to throw it on the gas soaked logs. A torrent of flame exploded out of the fireplace. Fortunately it did no lasting harm, but Ward didn't ask her to lay the fire again.

Fatima took pride in her appearance and was delighted to show up and smile at Sally with one, big, gold, front tooth. She had saved her wages to afford it. Then later she saved enough to do the second. Each took two weeks worth of her wages.

Fatima got a new pair of shoes that were too big, so she stuffed newspapers into them, determined to wear them anyway. She got blisters that became infected and resulted in angry red streaks that ran up her legs. Sally was very concerned and contacted a doctor she knew at the military base who provided her with penicillin to bring the infection under control. When Yvonne told Fatima that she should thank Sally for getting the medicine to cure the infection, Fatima said with assurance, "No. Inshallah." It was the will of Allah that she got better. There was no need to thank Sally or the penicillin.

Fatima threw overripe tomatoes over the railing and into the backyard, and they grew like Jack and the Beanstalk beans and produced marvelous multi-colored heirloom tomatoes.

Once two dogs somehow got into the courtyard and were copulating. Sally wanted them and their activity out of her courtyard, but she and Fatima couldn't get them to leave. Sally remembered what Ward had done with the cats in Alabama and found a firecracker. She was holding it and about to release it when it went off in her hand. It left a black coloring under the palm of her hand, and Fatima seemed to be deaf. Sally's first thought was, "Oh Dear! If she's deaf I will have to take care of her for the rest of her life." But to her relief the condition was temporary. Sally went to the base to have her hand cared for, and word quickly got around that Beightol's wife was out chasing mating dogs with a firecracker when the thing went off.

Fatima often heard the children singing the Sunday school song, "Yes, Jesus Loves Me." She asked Sally, "Does your Jesus love me?" Even though Sally had promised at her interview at Fort Hamilton never to speak of religion, she answered that yes, he did. Sally then put Fatima in touch with an English missionary, and Fatima became a Christian.

22 - Settling In

The whole first year they were in Morocco, the Beightols didn't have a telephone at home. Anything that came up, Sally had to manage if Ward was away. Fortunately, the September night Sally's water broke at two A.M. and she went into hard labor, Ward was at home. They had then been in Morocco for just three months. Yvonne was staying overnight as Sally's due date neared, so they woke her to tell her they were leaving. They raced for the hospital in Casablanca about an hour away. Sally asked Ward if he knew where the hospital was, and he replied that he'd flown over it once. The contractions by then were coming one upon the next, and Sally was beside herself. It very much looked as though Ward was going to have to use the aviation medicine skills he'd learned in his training in Alabama and stop the car to catch the baby. But they got to the gate of the hospital where a guard with a gun stopped them. Ward put the guard's hand on Sally's belly, and the guard quickly stepped aside to let them enter. Ward sped under the wing of a plane and aimed straight for the hospital. Sally was wheeled in, and with the third contraction, there was the baby. Sally clearly remembers the Black, military doctor who was in attendance for Karen's birth.

When Sally was back again in her big walled house with her three small children, an Arab tradesman arrived with wood that Ward had ordered for the fireplace. He unloaded it and came to Sally, wanting to be paid. Sally used her smatterings of languages to clarify that he would be paid by her husband - not by her. Sally was still not at all adept in matters of pounds, francs and kilos, and she knew this left her vulnerable to those who might see her as an easy mark. She had learned this the hard way, so she was determined not to fall prey again. The man scowled, loomed large and paced. At last, to Sally's great relief, Ward came home. Sally told Ward the amount the man was asking for. Ward looked at the firewood and got out his scale. The man said, "Weigh me." When he saw that the amount on the scale actually matched his weight, he said, "Okay. Give me a cigarette." Ward did, and the man shook his hand, accepting half of what he had originally asked.

Sally entertained for the general quite often. Ward would come home and ask if they could have 8 or 10 or 12 for supper. Sometimes there might be noteworthy guests such as the time Arthur Godfrey came for dinner when he was in Morocco. Whenever guests were coming, Sally would go to the Base Exchange to find what meat and staples were available. Nearly all of the food was shipped in from Germany, and Sally knew that being there when the ship unloaded was important if she was going to be able to feed her guests really well. But if she couldn't make it there in time, she could at least be sure to find a frozen turkey small enough for her oven or hamburger with which she could figure out many tasty options.

Fruits and vegetables would come from the open-air markets or sometimes be delivered to the house. Sally found the best way to wash them was in the bidet with a micro cleaner that killed germs because the Moroccans fertilized their crops with "night soil." The bidet was also the perfect place to bathe her kids. After the kids or the vegetables were scrubbed and clean, she would rinse them thoroughly in fresh water.

Their dinner guests were nearly always French, and Sally spoke almost no French, though Ward was fluent. Her recollection is that the French women dressed well, wore a lot of perfume and did not shave their legs or underarms. Sally played her role as the charming American hostess extremely well: preparing delicious fare and making pleasant conversation in her own patter which everyone seemed somehow to understand and appreciate. Ward, the quintessential interpreter and host, would roll his eyes and throw her a kiss with a wink. She was fancied something of the Unsinkable Molly Brown.

On only one occasion was Sally at an event that was hosted by the general's wife, the person in whose place Sally had been tapped to do the entertaining. The wife was much younger than the general but considerably older than Sally. She was his second wife, a former nurse, and rather retiring in social settings. Ward, Sally, and his crew of six guys had been invited for dinner. Sally was shocked and embarrassed for the general's wife when she saw that she had prepared only a single chicken to feed everyone – eight men and the two women. Sally grasped the significance of her role in creating an atmosphere of nurturing camaraderie, which supports the work everyone was doing for the common cause.

There was a garbage can outside the 8-foot wall that surrounded the house, and Sally realized that young Arab boys were scavenging its contents before the garbage collector emptied it. She regretted she'd been putting her coffee grounds carelessly over the top of the other food scraps, so she began packaging her leftovers to keep them cleaner and make them more accessible to anyone who could make use of them.

Young Arab boys monitoring the Beightol trash

As wonderful as the big house was with its gardens, it had no yard – no place where the kids could "go out and play." Ward and Sally talked it over and Ward was able to find another smaller but very nice place where they lived their last year in Morocco. It had a yard 150 feet deep and 100' wide with gardens on the front and side that Boaza maintained with exquisite care. He also took it upon himself to assure that no stranger glimpsed Sally in the yard in her shorts.

Sally was alarmed one day when she went into the yard where Yvonne was supervising the children. David and the little French boy who lived next door were playing cowboys and Indians. Sally went to Kristy who was playing near the wall, and was horrified to find that her baby daughter's little mouth was filled with snails she had been picking from the wall. Although they watched her with serious concern, the snails seemed to agree with Kristy, and she had no ill effects.

Sally was conscientious about the expected propriety of wearing a skirt and blouse that wasn't revealing when she went out in public.

Fatima even wore a veil over her face to run nearby to borrow something from their American neighbor.

Nonetheless, the weather was always swimming temperature, and a beach on the Mediterranean was close enough that they could see it from their first house as a strip of blue at the horizon. Going to the beach just made sense, especially since the Arab Moroccans didn't go to that beach at all, so the public clothing sensibilities didn't apply. Sally noted as an aside that the French bathing suits were even skimpier than the American ones. The French and the Americans, however, were never at the beach at the same time. By some unwritten rule, the French didn't go to the beach until after 3:00, while the Americans went in the morning. Sally would pack peanut butter and jelly sandwiches. Her friend Shirley Cheney whose husband Newt was a pilot and friend of Ward's, would pack her own kids into her car and pick up Sally and her kids, and they would all head to the beach. Shirley's kids called Kristy "Kiki," and the pet name stuck for a long time. The Americans had the entire beach to themselves until 3:00 when they all went home for a nap.

Sally and Kristy at the beach

Ward with Newt Cheney at the beach in spear fishing gear

One day Ward, Newt Cheney and three of their bachelor, Air Force friends were off duty. They decided it would be fun to take to the beach a big, sturdy, military raft they had acquired. Shirley Cheney and Sally joined them, having left the kids at home with nursemaids. Around noon the guys launched the raft and clambered in, each with a paddle. Sally and Shirley waved and watched as the raft moved further out from shore. Then as they sunned, swam and chatted, the raft continued to move further and further away until it was out of sight.

Sally and Shirley assured each other that surely these experienced, adult, military men could take care of themselves. But by 2 o'clock, the men had not returned, and impatience was setting in. By 3 o'clock, impatience had turned to anger as the sun moved down the sky. It was clearly time to go home. By 4 o'clock they were scared and consumed with worry. Something must have happened. What should they do? What could they do? Were they already widows? Widows alone with small children in Africa? They paced the beach, occasionally catching each other's eye as they wordlessly pondered their fate.

Finally, it was after six and twilight when they spotted the familiar shapes of their guys coming into view across the beach. Caught in a jumble of relief, gratitude and rage, the women rushed to them. Even in the fading light they could see they were covered with scrapes and contusions.   They explained that they had paddled too far out. Then a current took them and carried them for miles down the coast as the beach disappeared in the distance. They were at the mercy of the current until the raft finally collided with a rocky reef. It punctured the raft, and it could no longer hold them. They had to swim through the sharp, coral reefs as they finally made their way to shore. They found their way to a road and found they were perhaps 20 miles from where they'd started. There was nothing to do but start hitch hiking.

Only when Sally and Ward were back in the car and the whole ordeal was over did her tears come, and then she sobbed.

After the ordeal, the Beightols were immensely glad to be able to resume their normal lives. Once again, evenings were especially enjoyable. The family would picnic with friends in the Beightol backyard around a fire. Someone would bring a guitar, and there would be singing, story telling, laughter and discussions of matters great and small as they basked in each other's company, sometimes until dawn. The men invented a ridiculous ongoing challenge. Each would put a burning candle on either fender of their little French cars and see who could drive the farthest without the candles going out. Ward and Sally would watch them go up the street and hear their laughter in the distance.

Sometimes they had opportunities to explore Morocco. The ancient wells with their simple but ingenious engineering especially intrigued Ward. The architecture, the landmarks, and the people were always breathtakingly new to them.

They saw Berbers who refer to themselves as Amazigh. They are descendants of the native people who have lived in Morocco since the Stone Age. The men were usually dressed in long blue robes, and the women carried bundles on their heads and their babies wrapped in slings around their bodies. Each child had a little topknot of hair for Allah to "grab them up to heaven" if he chose. In their travels they would often see women threshing wheat by hand in fields by the road.

Many Arabs were superstitious about cameras and quickly ducked or hid so that their spirits couldn't be captured and trapped in the little black boxes. Ward became adept at spotting a good subject for a picture and then turning away from it before quickly turning back to snap it before the subject had an opportunity to duck.

On a few treasured occasions, Ward and Sally were able to make arrangements for their kids to be cared for so that they could get away with friends for several days of vacation.

The bullfights in Spain

They attended the bullfights across the Straits of Gibraltar in Spain where they had a wonderfully memorable time. In their hats and sunglasses, the group had a picture taken. Then twenty-five years later after they had all retired, they reunited in the Cayman Islands and posed for a new picture in exactly the same positions that they had been sitting at the bull fights.

Watching the bullfights

The bullfight watchers 25 years later in the Caymans

On another occasion, Ward and Sally drove to Marakech with Bernice and Chuck Weiss in the Weiss's little MG. (Sally would discover that Chuck, a medical doctor, had actually grown up near her in Ann Arbor.)

The roads were in extremely poor condition, and the driving was "pretty crazy. It was as though donkey cart drivers had been put behind the steering wheels of the cars." The MG had flat tire after flat tire, and there were no new tires to be had anywhere, nor were there garages to buy parts or find repairmen. So each time Ward and Chuck would have too choice but to hop out and patch the tires. Nonetheless, they had a wonderful time. They stayed in a lovely hotel and ate in its lovely restaurant and enjoyed the sites and the shopping. In the souk in

Marrakech Sally saw mounds of roasted grasshoppers being sold as tasty crisp treats.

They'd been in Morocco for about a year when Sally heard gunshots. She was at home with the kids and Ward was at work. Word reached her that the Arabs were trying to claim their independence from France – that the revolution was underway. Sentries were posted outside the gates of their house, and Sally was cautioned not to go outside. It was safe, however, for Fatima who was an Arab to come and go.

The rebels were initially successful and did wrest control from the French for several weeks, but they could not maintain it. But the French saw the writing on the wall and agreed to negotiate a settlement and accede to Morocco's independence. America worked at establishing stable relations with the new government, and life on the surface resumed a reasonable and fairly orderly tone.

Whatever compelling concerns Ward was privy to, he didn't talk much about them when he was at home.

The French wives, however, sometimes felt conspicuous and vulnerable in public. They asked Ward to chaperone them on errands if anti-French tensions might run high. He would tease, "So Sal, I'm going to pick up some French ladies this afternoon."

"Have a good time," she'd wave. For Sally, the next year and a half felt as though it picked up where it left off before those first shots. And Sally kept her fingers crossed that Ward would remain safe.

23 - It felt like "*A Thousand and One Nights*"

Sally, Ward and five other couples attended a feast at the home of a Moroccan gentleman in appreciation of the efforts of Don Norland of the American diplomatic corps making it possible for the Moroccan's son to attend the University of Nebraska. Don and Ward were friends, and Don had invited Ward, Sally, and several other colleagues and their wives to join him for this celebratory event.

The home was truly stunning. The entryway was domed with a ceiling of colored glass like the Alhambra that diffused wonderful patterns of light onto the terrazzo floor. The guests were escorted to a room on the right and seated on cut-velvet poofs in intense primary colors while a darling young girl of about eleven, one of the gentlemen's daughters, washed each guest's hands in a ritual of welcome. The young girl, her clothing, the rooms, and the welcoming ritual washing all made Sally feel as if she had slipped back into the time of the Bible or "A Thousand and One Nights" or the Alhambra.

Sally and the other guests were escorted to another large and beautifully appointed room and seated again on great comfortable poofs of cut velvet. The sons of the host were young and handsome and took seats among the American and English guests. The sons spoke French, so Ward was able to interpret for those who spoke English but no French. Servants carried in enormous round trays of food and placed them before the guests on a long, low table. There was lamb, turkey with red and other lovely sauces, and couscous. The host used a sharp blade that looked like a saber to slish slash the meat into smaller portions. Everyone ate using their right hands only. (The left hand was reserved for "nature" which meant "bathrooming.") For couscous and the sweet delicacies that came later for desert, right hands were used to roll bite-sized pieces into balls or to break off portions before putting them into their mouths.

The guests adjourned to a separate room for the traditional three cups of tea, and hookah pipes were brought in for the men to use later. Though the tea was sweet and hot, it was not served in cups but in small flowered glasses that Sally observed for all the world looked exactly like the Kraft Foods glasses that Kraft cheese was sold in at home.. The temperature of the tea was just right so that the glasses weren't too hot to hold.

The gentleman asked if the women would like to meet his wife, and see his home, and they were, of course, happy to do so. He clapped his hands and a veiled woman instantly appeared whom he introduced as his wife but who must have been his first wife since it became clear that there must also have been other wives as well. She removed her veil only when they were completely away from the men.

With the women gone, the pipe was passed from one to the next, but Ward passed it on, a bit concerned about what it was they might be smoking. And he was not a smoker.

The host's wife was soft spoken and knew little English, but the women reached out to understand her. Sally was excited when she understood that they were going to see the master bedroom, and she envisioned something exotic and timeless like the rest of the house. It did have wonderful linens embroidered with white on white, but what they saw instead of exotic was the new, modern, French bedroom suite the wife had just acquired and was clearly very proud of.

Sally's observant eyes also noticed that the vase holding flowers beside the bed was merely a glass milk bottle like the kind that were delivered with cream on the top when she was a girl in Ann Arbor. They moved onto the roof that was a large, secluded, outdoor, living space surrounded by a wall. Amidst the benches and flowers they met the family's other smiling polite children, who ranged in all skin tones from very dark to very light. It seemed clear they had multiple mothers, but no one felt it proper to ask.

Sally was surprised to see a regular, rope, clothesline perhaps 20 feet long that extended off in a second direction as well. All along it the most beautiful clothing had been hung, apparently for the admiration of the guests. Garments were hung with clothespins from the shoulders so they showed to best advantage. It was all quite amazing.

24 - Flying Side Trips With the General

Ward piloted General Hutchinson whenever and wherever he needed or chose to go. Their plane was a propeller-driven Gooney Bird, and he was assisted by a copilot, navigator and other crew if needed. On rare occasions, General Hutchinson chose to get away for R & R.

The general planned big-game hunting safari south in the continent. His safari was indeed a success, and the satisfied general had porters haul back two rhinoceros heads which he planned to take back to Rabat to have mounted for display. Captain Beightol was responsible for transporting the detached, bloody, stinky, maggot-filled heads in the plane that he took such pride in. But in military matters, the general was the general, and his word was law. They flew the "trophies" back to Rabat and then fumigated the plane.

On another occasion, General Hutchinson informed Ward that they were flying to Spain to buy fur coats where the prices were thought to be far more reasonable than in the United States. While the general considered one coat and another, Ward thought about how fine Sally would look in a fur. He picked out a silver stole and negotiated what he thought was a bargain price for it. He was excited to be bringing it home as a surprise to Sally.

Sally was indeed pleased as she wrapped the fur around her shoulders and asked Ward what kind of fur it was. He replied he thought it was mink. Sally shook her head no, she didn't think so. Nonetheless, she thoroughly enjoyed wearing it, and they referred to it as her "slink."

After they returned to America, she took it to a furrier for cold storage and asked incidentally, what type of fur it was. The man said with a smile, "Yes, this stole is made from the underbelly of muskrats." Its price, she discovered, would be almost exactly what Ward had paid for it.

On yet another occasion, the general, Ward, and a crew ended up at the Necchi sewing machine factory in Italy. The company's new zigzag sewing machine had just come out, and knowing what a skillful seamstress Sally was, Ward bought her the new model. When they boarded the plane, they found there were mechanical problems that would keep it grounded. The general, Ward and the crew were forced to make their way back to Rabat using public transportation.

Necchi sewing machines are famously well made and *very* heavy. Ward had no choice but to hoist and trundle, drag and maneuver the machine all the way back to Rabat. It was New Year's Eve when Ward, the general and the crew got back to Rabat. The Beightols had been invited to a party, and after they arrived, Sally looked at Ward and realized he had turned an astonishing shade of yellow. She quickly took him to the infirmary where he was diagnosed with hepatitis that he must have contracted on the trip. His condition became increasingly serious, and he was taken to the hospital in Casablanca, an hour away, where he stayed for a month.

Sally was driving to visit Ward one day with another young military wife who was pregnant and going to the same hospital. Suddenly the sky turned dark as thousands of frantically moving things of some kind started pummeling the car and smashing and splattering against the windshield. Sally had trouble seeing with so many on the windshield and turned on the windshield wipers, but that made them squish and platter everywhere. Were they grasshoppers??? The sight of the oozing insect bodies made Sally's pregnant companion sick to her stomach. But stopping to let her vomit outside in the onslaught was unthinkable, so there was nothing to do but stay in the reeking car as Sally tried to inch the car blindly forward as her companion threw up. After what felt like an eternity, the cloud then quickly dissipated and was gone as quickly as it had come.

The wipers cleared enough of the mess so that Sally could see, and they made their way to the hospital. After regaling sick Ward with the fascinating but disgusting details, they settled for a visit before it was time to return to Rabat. When they reached the site of their disastrous earlier encounter, the swarm had passed, and what was left was only a slippery slush of grasshoppers on the road.

When Ward was well again, he and Sally eagerly opened the sewing machine case he had struggled so strenuously to bring to her. To their great disappointment, they found that the machine was broken. They located the instruction manual only to open it and discover it was entirely written in Italian. Ward could have managed it in French, but Italian was another story. Eventually they did locate a manual in English that allowed them to get the machine repaired. Then one day at the Base Exchange, Sally spotted the very same machine. Curious, she went to check out its price, and to her chagrin, she saw the price was exactly what Ward had paid for it, but it wasn't broken. And its manual was in English.

25 - Back to the United States

In 1955 after two and a half years, the general's tour in Morocco ended, and the five Beightols returned to the United States. It was 80 degrees in Morocco when they boarded the military aircraft with its canvas seats and headed for New Jersey.

The little girls wore shiny, red, patent leather Mary Janes on their feet. It was early April, and winter had not yet released its grip on New Jersey when they stepped from the plane onto the snowy tarmac. The little girls' feet slid out from under them, and they went tumbling in shock and tears. Before long Sally who was six months pregnant also found herself in tears when Ward made an offhand, admiring comment about an attractive young woman passing on the street.

They were anxious to be on with the next phase of their lives back in the United States, but then they found they would have to wait another week or so until their car arrived from Morocco on a later ship. It was a painful time of adjusting to their new reality which did not include Morocco's easy climate, its ready domestic help in caring for the children, and the extremely reasonable cost of food. They were shocked to find that even buying hamburgers for the family at a restaurant in America cost a fortune, but they had no means of cooking for themselves. It was not an easy beginning.

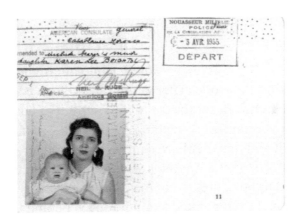

Passport with the third little Beightol,
Karen

26 - Lincoln, Nebraska

Ward's new orders were to report to the Strategic Air Command Base in Lincoln, Nebraska. The first thing that struck Ward and Sally when they were finally in their car and on their way to Nebraska was how colorful the cars were. When they'd left the U.S, cars were dark, the most exotic being a light blue like the one they owned. But now there were turquoises, golds, whites, brilliant reds, silvers, and sometimes even hot pinks or chartreuses. And many were in two-tones.

The Beightols began a search to locate a house they could make into their new home. They discovered a big red brick one with a ten-foot wide porch at 2127 Harwood. It had a spacious yard with room for a garden, and a large garage. And the asking price fit their budget. However, the reasons for the low asking price became readily apparent: the grounds were completely overgrown; the interior was filthy; everything seemed in need of repair or replacement. Nonetheless, they could see that with work they'd be able to make it into a great home that would work very well for them. They put in an offer that was accepted.

2127 Harwood

It made most sense financially to simply camp out in the house as they got underway with the work. After getting the kids to bed the first night, Sally reached into the closet for the nightgown she'd hung there. She slipped it on and could feel something moving - a cockroach was crawling from it and onto her bare skin. With a shudder of horror, she stifled a scream, lest she alarm the kids. So in addition to everything else that needed to be addressed in the house, when they pulled down cupboards that had been painted shut, the space behind them was encrusted with cockroaches. Ward actually called the former owners to chide them that they'd left something behind that he thought they might want to come and claim. Maybe they wanted to come and collect their cockroaches? The man laughed awkwardly, declined and as quickly as possible got off the phone.

They removed everything they could and had the fumigators come. Once that was complete and the bugs were gone, they installed new cupboards, refinished the floors, painted and carpeted. They restored the neglected recreation room in the basement and reestablished the lost character of the wonderful old house. Ward's brothers Willis and Bob came to help with the interior painting. They sang as they painted and dubbed themselves "The Chem Tones." There was a great big garage and a garden and yard that they transformed with love and attention. All four corners of the second floor were bedrooms, and each was distinctive. One was for the parents; one was a sun porch that was also the nursery for Pam; David had his own room; and Kristy and Karen shared. There was a perfect spot that the kids would call "The Christmas Room" where Sally would place their Christmas trees the years they were in Lincoln.

Ed and Sue's wedding with David, center front, as ring bearer and Karen to his right and Kristy to his left

Sally's brother Ed married his wife Sue in 1955 just after Sally and her family returned from Morocco. Sue was a lovely girl he had dated in high school who had gone on to become a nurse while Ed earned his degree in Hotel and Restaurant Management at Michigan State. Sally remembers the happy events of their wedding and in particular how adorable her own little girls were as part of the wedding party in the beautiful white organdy dresses Sally had made for the event. She had added fancy, lime-green stitching along the hemlines

93

with her Necchi sewing machine, and each dress had a lime green bow at the waist. "They were darling." And David was the handsome ring bearer.

Ed was friendly, capable and outgoing, a natural salesman like his father, and with his degree he readily found good jobs in the industry. Ed and Sue's first child Mary Ellen was about the same age as Ward and Sally's last child, Ralph. Then came daughters Sharie and Joanna before their son John.

27 - The Kids at 2127 Harwood

Life in the big house on Harwood Street was always percolating with kid activity. Sally had one core principle that she believed was essential for her children to internalize: " Always be responsible for your actions." Given that, she was happy to watch them develop as "free range kids" who chose what they wanted to do, experimented like the little scientists that kids are, and relied on themselves and each other. There was always someone to play with, laugh with, cry with, or sing with. And managing the easy equilibrium was always mom. Sally says she hardly ever said no to her kids' ideas, and when Ward got home, he loved playing with the kids as well.

David, Kristy, Karen and Pam

Amazingly, Sally said, the kids got along together remarkably well. Early on she established one of her few rules: "If you're going to fuss, you must fuss in a whisper." The reason was, she said, that if they didn't fuss in a whisper, she would think that they were trying to get her attention. If they wanted to settle it themselves, they had to whisper. And to this day the sisters may find themselves whispering when they consider various sides of an issue. But now they also appreciate and accept that each is a unique and strong individual entitled to her own perspectives and opinions.

Sally laughed at a cartoon her friend Pat Scott sent her. In the cartoon the playpen was in the middle of the room, and the mama, not one of the kids, was in the playpen. There she sat, reading the paper while the kids played in the room around her and would come and hang over the sides to talk with her and show her things. Sally laughs ruefully, asking why she didn't think of this herself?!

With four little kids under the age of six, someone was always in some stage of potty training. Sally discovered that she could facilitate the process by engaging the kids' desire for autonomy. She showed the kids where the dry underpants were kept in the bottom drawer at just their level. If they had an accident, Sally would say, "Oh, dear. You'll have to go and change," and she would help them take the soiled undies to the diaper pail. They would then go to get dry ones from the drawer to put on. Everyone knew or was learning the routine, and the kids that were a bit older modeled it for the younger, and training didn't take long.

Karen, however, added a new level of ingenuity to the process. Sally noticed she was on her way out the door, and Sally asked where she was going. "Kay's house," Karen replied. Kay's house was next door. And then Karen would be back before long. Some time later she'd again be on her way out the door. "Where are you going?" "Kay's house." Sally finally discovered that at Kay's house, their potty chair was down low, but at Sally's it was up high on the toilet. Independent Karen preferred not to have to ask for help. Sally invested in a low potty.

Busy little Karen showed her initiative whenever she had an opportunity. One morning Sally came down to find her curled up in the middle of the table with the toaster and a loaf of bread. "I cook toast," she explained and indicated with dignity the whole loaf she'd done.

The kids found the idea of washing dishes fascinating, and so Sally found step stools and let them wash the dishes. They made a terrible mess, but they had a wonderful time.

The ten-foot wide front porch was one of their favorite places. They played "office" by the hour with the junk mail they collected and made clothes and hats for their troll dolls with pieces of fabric Sally gave them.

One of Sally's other rules was "If Mama works, then we all work. If Mama plays, then we all play." And if you work, you work hard. And if you play, you play hard. So when Kristy decided it would be wonderful if she and Sally had matching dresses they could wear when they went to events together, Sally agreed, but with the understanding that if she was working on Kristy's dress, then Kristy needed to be cleaning the house. So the little girl cleaned as Sally sewed her yellow gingham dress with tucks and lace. Kristy always felt so proud when she and her mom wore their matching "Sissy Dresses." And Sally made for all the girls and herself matching dresses out of a delightful beige fabric with cute little pink and white pigs. The kids called them their "piggy dresses." They adored them.

Sally and Ward established early on with their kids that it was a cause for happiness if something wonderful happened for one of them. Perhaps one and not the others was invited to a birthday party. "This time it may not be your time, but we will all be happy with you when your time comes too." So there was no hovering effort to compensate so everything always felt equal.

There was also an established joke in the family when the kids might be pushing the limits and Ward would call them to task. "Now don't hit them in the head!" Sally would say in mock warning, and the kids knew it was time to back off.

David, who pressed the limits more than his sisters, once was mouthing off, and Sally turned to give him a playful swat with her left hand, but to her horror caught his lip with her ring and split it open. She felt dreadful when she saw that she had inadvertently drawn her beloved son's blood.

Sally, like typical, American mothers in the 1950s, sent her children "out to play." The rule was that if the kids weren't going to be in the yard or on the porch, they needed to let Sally know where they would be. One morning Sally came downstairs and found a note on the refrigerator from David and Kristy. The note read:

GONE TO THE PARK

(signed) HANSEL AND GRETEl

Kristy and David had great fun together, and Kristy was the one who was always furthest up the tree or the one leading the charge.

To curb her kids' natural inclination to come back in again and again after they'd gone out to play, Sally added a new rule. You could only come in if you were bleeding. Years later David said he thought it was mean for his mom to have such a rule, but the sisters instantly countered, "Oh David. Mom was kidding. She meant it to be funny."

Pam remembers playing next door when she got her hand caught in an old car door. Her little finger was torn and bleeding when she came home sobbing. Sally comforted her, did first aid on the injured finger and assured her little daughter that it would be fine by the time she got married. Pam told Sally recently, "It was the only lie you ever told me." Pam said she could still see the scar when she got married.

Seven o'clock was bedtime for the children at the Beightol house. It was filled with baths and songs and stories. They sang, "White Coral Bells, "Fairies Have Never a Penny to Spend," "Swing Low, Sweet Chariot," "Dites Moi" and many others. But by summer, the days were long and the sunsets late. Kristy complained to her mom, "But it's still light out, and I'm not tired."

"But I am," Sally replied with a kiss.

Right across the street from their house was the school all the kids would attend when they were old enough. David was the only one of school age when they arrived in Lincoln. He was in kindergarten. Sally prepared him for his first day, and off he went to the school across the street. She watched and waved as he entered the school. But then she got a call from the school saying that David wasn't there. How could that be? Sally went out to look, and there was David sitting on the curb playing with the leaves. Sally asked why he was there and not in school. He said, "I needed to see the leaves. They are so pretty." Sally admired them and asked David to pick some for his teacher. With David holding the leaf bouquet, they found his classroom. The teacher was wonderful. When David and Sally explained about the leaves, the teacher looked at the leaves David had brought her and said, "Oh yes, David! The leaves are so beautiful!" And she built on the opportunity for learning David had offered and took the children outside to enjoy and learn from the leaves. Kindergarten was a wonderful year.

But in first grade things were different. When Sally asked her bright, artistic son to describe his teacher, he said matter-of-factly, "She's beige." The teacher summoned David's mother to school, saying David was a problem: He spoke without being called on and disrupted the class. Sally should come and witness the behavior her son was demonstrating. Sally tried to slip inconspicuously into the back of the room to witness, but the sharp-eyed David spotted her and jumped to his feet like a small perfect host and announced, "Oh, Miss Elbert and boys and girls! This is my mother. Let me introduce you." The scowling teacher said afterward, "Now you see what I mean!" It was a long year.

In third grade, David was *over the moon* that he was going to learn to play the piano the Beightols had recently acquired. He eagerly devoured the lessons and then ALL the time. He wouldn't stop. After becoming adept at the piano, he went on t to learn to play every stringed instrument.

In Lincoln, Ward was with SAC, the Strategic Air Command, and as a result was gone a great deal of the time. He was either flying, or on-call at the base, or traveling to Europe for periods of up to a month, or teaching a course to airmen about how to manage nuclear weapons and if necessary how to detonate "big boy and little boy," the atomic bombs.

Ward used the family car for work, so they purchased a little, gray, clunker Pontiac that would allow Sally to run to the grocery store and do errands. Then she started getting provocative phone calls in which a man's creepy voice would ask things like, "Are you tall and good looking?" She would snap, "No. I'm short and fat" and slam down the phone. She called the police who told her."Those kind of guys are usually harmless,. They almost always are just talkers. They almost never showed up. With Ward gone and she alone so much of the time with her kids, this was not entirely comforting.

One day Ward was gone when a gangly man dressed all in green appeared at her door looking "as though he'd crawled out from under a rock." Sally spoke to him through the screen. He began with a few wheedling questions, and then in the creepiest possible terms, informed her that he'd come to buy sex.

The fiery rage that surged through her core shocked even her. She pulled herself to her full 5'9"and rained such vitriol on him that he trembled, turned and bolted for his car.

Still shaking, Sally called her neighbor who jumped in his car and did his best to chase after and catch the guy, but he had disappeared. Sally called the police. They told her that other similar reports had now come to their attention, and they were actively looking for him. Shortly afterward, they notified her that they'd found and arrested the predator. It turned out that he was a former employee of the Department of Motor Vehicles. Perhaps he'd spotted her at the grocery store and noted the license plate number of her car. Then he had tracked her address through the department's records. The family ever after referred to him with a shudder as "Mr. Green."

Once Ward had been gone for a month when he got word that he needed to report to Washington, D.C. for three more months. Sally wasted no time in finding an older German couple happy to live in the house and maintain it while they were gone. Ward made arrangements for a place for them to stay in Washington, D.C. It turned out to be a third floor walk up without an elevator. Trundling kids and groceries up the stairs felt quite challenging enough, and Ward decided to give up beer because dragging it up the stairs seemed ridiculous. Between the exercise the stairs provided and deleting beer from his diet, he lost 30 pounds and was looking quite buff by the time they returned to Lincoln. Sally and the kids made the most of Washington, D.C.

Ward was sworn to secrecy about the nature of the work he was doing there. Sally was warned never to let the children outside to play alone, and she was required to let Ward off at a designated location from which he would be met by men with guns and escorted to a designated location. Decades would pass before Ward disclosed to Sally that what they were doing involved plans to be implemented if America lost the Cold War.

Back in Lincoln, Ward resumed his professional duties with the Air Force as well as the work he did in support of the Lincoln community. He was deep]y involved in working to improve the justice system for juveniles.

March 6, 1959

TO WHOM IT MAY CONCERN:

Over the past several weeks the Lincoln Community Council has, through its Juvenile Court Committee, devoted considerable time in study of Nebraska's juvenile court laws. This work has required a great deal of time and effort on the part of all participants.

Captain Beightol has served on this Committee from its inception and has contributed substantially of his time not only in meetings but in study and research of problems encountered. His professional manner and approach has gained for him the deserved respect of his associates. His sincere interest in civic affairs in this community has not only led to his acceptance as a substantial and responsible member of the community but has had the broader effect of cultivating the understanding that Air Force personel generally possess an attitude of responsibility toward civic affairs.

As Chairman of the Committee upon which he has served, I know that the officers of the Lincoln Community Council are counting on Captain Beightol for future service.

Sincerely,

Sally and Ward also incorporated fun into their lives and their children's lives whenever and wherever they could. Ward was a gifted vocalist and entertainer. At the Officers Club, he and Sally were pivotal in producing a gala talent show in which Sally was the master of ceremonies, and Ward performed in many musical numbers . There were with all kinds of elegant costume changes.

Ward enjoyed the intellectual challenge and competition of the game of bridge, while Sally loved its social aspects but was lukewarm about the game itself - until in Lincoln she found a book that explained the essence of bridge. That's when she had the Ah Ha! moment that suddenly clarified the mathematical nature and challenges of the game in terms she all at once *got*. Her fascination grew, and she set up a regular couples duplicate bridge club with three and then four tables. In the immediate neighborhood after the kids were in bed, the nearby neighbors often spontaneously got together to play bridge, running home at intervals to check on the kids.

When she was growing up, Sally, her parents and the family's friends would spend part of each summer at a lake near Ann Arbor where one highlight each year would be creating a movie. It would involve Indians, their chief, bonfires and papooses. So when the Beightols were in Lincoln, Sally suggested that they should make a neighborhood movie. She and her neighbor wrote the script and described the costumes everyone would wear. The setting was an orphanage, and the Beightol house was to be the orphanage. They titled the movie *Progress is Our Most Important Product*. It had characters Patience, Prudence and Progress, the baby. Mary Ann Maxer, who was a former runner- up for the title of Mrs. Nebraska, was to be "the good girl," while, of course, Sally was "the bad girl" who in the end gives birth to the baby named Progress. The "doctor" was to wear a white coat, and everyone was to come in costume. They filmed one whole Saturday and ended with a picnic on the porch with all the orphans. Everyone felt pleased and proud, Their production had involved everyone, and it was so much fun!

'PAN MAN DAN' PARADES

an the Pan Man" David Beightol, son ... down South St. as part of that area's
ipt. and Mrs. Ward Beightol of 2127 ... postponed Centennial parade. (Star P
ood, jangles his wagon of wares

David "the Pan Man" in the Lincoln parade

Ward's brother Bob lived in Omaha, only about 50 miles away. There he raised golden retrievers as a hobby and was eager to gift his brother and his family with one of his wonderful pups. The family named their new pet "Lady Kitty Kelly of Lakewood," which allowed them the joy of calling, "Here, kitty kitty," and having a happy golden retriever come bounding to the call.

28 - Bertha Beightol

At some point Bertha came into the Beightol fold. She was a tall, angular, rawboned girl who'd grown up on a farm and was enrolled in secretarial school. Her mother had given her a frizzy home permanent that did nothing to enhance her appearance.

In return for room at board, she was to help Sally with the kids and the house much as Fatima had done in Morocco. Sally asked what she liked to have for breakfast, and to Sally's astonishment, she answered, "tomato soup," canned Campbell's tomato soup, and that's what they got for her

The arrangement worked out well, and she lived with the Beightols for about three years. She was wonderful with the kids and a great help to Sally. The kids called her "Bertha Beightol."

One night Sally heard crying when she went past Bertha's room. She knocked and asked Bertha what was wrong. Bertha said she could come in, and she asked Sally, "How do I meet people like you and the friends who come to your house? Your life is so different from life with my family. They are so strict. With your family almost every meal is a party." Bertha was realizing that her mother didn't want any more for her daughter than the life she herself had known.

Sally advised her gently, "Sometimes, Bertha, you must make difficult decisions. Sometimes you must do what your mind and heart tell you you must do, even if it means breaking away from your family." After Bertha finished secretarial school and left the Beightols, she continued her education and became a teacher.

Bertha was the reason Sally discovered she was actually a very good bowler. With Bertha watching the kids, Sally was free to bowl with the "military ladies." She carried a 185 average and once bowled five strikes in a row in a tournament. She made the newspapers and had a bracelet with 50 charms representing strikes she had made.

One day she was leaving the bowling alley and passed the young pin setters who were in a cluster. She heard a long, low, wolf whistle and was internally smiling to herself, "I'm in my late twenties, and I've

Happy Gal ... Collects Strike

Sally the bowler

Within the image (handwritten and clipping text):

You finally got your picture in the paper. 1960 - January

Could this be Sally

Guess Who

A Friend

Beightol Is Tops In LAFB Tourney

Sally Beightol's 1655-pin aggregate carried off top honors in the all events competition at the Lincoln Air Force Base's Women's bowling tournament.

Mrs. Beightol's 547 scratch score also copped first place in singles competition.

Other winners:

still got it!" when one of them said, "She would have been okay in her day"

"Oh yes," she thought, "Pride goeth before a fall."

And then Sally was pregnant - again. No matter what birth control method they employed, and they employed them all, Sally always got pregnant. An OBGYN finally told her she was a "double ovulator." It seems Sally and Ward were destined to have the wonderful big family they had. Ralph was born in 1960. Though their plan was for two children, they'd arrived in Lincoln with three, and now were leaving with five.

29 - K. I. Sawyer Air Force Base

Ward, Sally, five kids and Kitty, the dog, piled into their car for the nearly 800 mile winter trip to K.I. Sawyer Air Force Base in the Upper Peninsula of Michigan. The base was about two hours from where Sally's mother Minnie had grown up in the Keweenaw. Because of its proximity to Lake Superior, the area receives many feet of lake effect snow each year.

The Beightols were to live on the base, but their place was not yet ready, so it was necessary for them to rent an interim place for several months. They found a new small house across a not too busy road from Lake Superior, and Ward commuted to the base. The family enjoyed their time there, meeting people and hiking around the lake. As part of SAC, Ward initially did some flying at K.I. Sawyer, but his appointment as Assistant Director of Personnel quickly turned into Director of Personnel, and the job consumed most of his time. He especially enjoyed the work because it allowed him to utilize his academic background in Psychology to the benefit of the young men at the base.

Ward with his boys, David and baby Ralph

After several months of living out of boxes and with Christmas coming, their house on the base was still not ready. Sally had to let the kids know that they were simply not going to be able to have a regular Christmas this year. Sally explained that all of their stockings and ornaments and gifts were some place in storage. It didn't make sense to have a Christmas tree, but she assured them they would have fun anyway. It was just the way it was. The kids were deeply disappointed, but David and Kristy, 11 and 9 years old, took matters into their own hands and appeared at the door proudly dragging a sizable pine tree. Sally was speechless! Where had this come from? It turns out that they had found some sharp tools stored on the property and had also spotted a very nice pine right in the front yard. It was the focal point of the landscaping for the house, and the two of them had proudly felled it. So they did have a Christmas tree that first year in Michigan, a very nice and very expensive Christmas tree. They needed to pay for a landscaper to replace it with another comparably large tree. But the kids had a wonderful time making paper chains, stringing popcorn and cranberries and making gifts for each other. They remember it fondly as one of their favorite Christmases ever, and it brought back for Ward reminiscences of the Webster City Christmases of his own childhood.

The family finally moved onto the base and loved it. All the kids but little Ralph were in school and required far less oversight. Sally said she didn't micromanage her kids with their schoolwork. If they didn't do it, they were responsible for facing the consequences. Sometimes one or another might complain that they weren't feeling well or drag their feet about going to school. Sally would say, "Oh good! Stay home. We'll bake cookies!" Most often they replied with authority, "No, Mom,

I have to go to school." Sally says that whether her approach was right or wrong, all of her kids went on to attend college and lead responsible, productive lives.

When summer came to upper Michigan there were wild blueberries everywhere. Sally would send the kids out with cups and tell them that when they'd gathered four cups, they would make a pie. It would take them only 10 minutes.

Kitty, their wonderful golden retriever, loved K.I Sawyer. She was very bright,

David with Ralph on his shoulders

and Sally could ask, "Kitty, where's the baby?" And Kitty would point at Ralph, wherever he was. Kitty would sit on the front porch and wait for the kids to come home on the school bus that stopped on the corner outside the house.

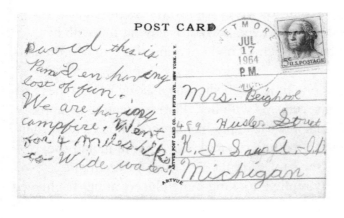

Pam's postcard from camp

When the four older kids all went to camp, Kitty was miserable, refused to eat or drink, and moped in great depression until they returned.

Kitty was a wonderful dog but also a hopeless thief. She loved nothing more than bringing presents home. She brought a graduated set of metal mixing bowls one at a time over a period of days. She brought roasting pans and giant teddy bears and would leave them on the doorstep. Sometimes the gifts were smelly and nasty, but one time Kitty outdid herself. She proudly came hope with Colonel Handy's gold shoes which a neighbor watched Kitty swipe. She smiled, "Kitty's the only thief I know."

The winter returned with tons of snow, and it was very cold. David built a slope in the backyard, and the kids sledded and experimented with skiing. Then they took lessons and could ski out the door right to the rope tow.

30 - Putting Sally's Hobbies to Greater Use

But because of the long winter isolation, many of the military wives on the base grew bored and stir crazy. As a result, Ward noted, there was an increasing exodus of wives who were leaving their husbands. In the meantime, however, Sally was having fun with her new hobby of making hats for herself and covering shoes to coordinate with outfits.

Sally remembers one time when she was making hats in the basement Pam who was seven was with her. Pam was eating an apple and had begun poking pins into the apple like a pincushion. Then when she took a bite she realized the bite she took had a pin in it, and she swallowed it. Alarmed, she said, "Mama, I just swallowed a pin." "No. You couldn't have," Sally replied, looking more closely at her frightened daughter. "Oh yes, I did." So Pam ended up in the hospital until they were sure it had passed through her system without harming her.

As Director of Personnel, Ward was concerned about morale on the base and asked Sally if she might be able to teach a class to the women at the base on some of the things she did. "Well, sure," she replied, and her offer brought 30 responses.

Sally had been getting her supplies mail order through a company in Chicago whose owner referred to himself as "Seymour the Fox." Sally purchased the supplies for the ladies in her new class from Seymour and sold them to the ladies for what she had paid for them. Everyone had a wonderful time creating hats that first class and were eager to sign up for her next class too. They made cloche hats with pheasant feathers and straw hats for the spring employing beautiful fabrics. Sally arranged a hat show for the Officers' Wives Club. This recruited even more eager students, and she ordered more supplies from Seymour the Fox. This marked the very beginning of a new direction her life would take.

Sally decided a Greenbrier van manufactured by Chevrolet would be the perfect vehicle for her family. It offered seats for all the kids and plenty of space for transporting stuff. It was the only car that she ordered totally by herself.

Sally and her hat creations

During the years since they'd all returned from Africa, Sally had kept in touch with their good friends Bernice and Chuck Weiss with whom they had shared such memorable times in Morocco. The Weisses lived in Ann Arbor and invited Sally to visit, suggesting she could see her parents at the same time. Ward wasn't able to get away, but Sally was able to make arrangements for the three younger kids to stay at home and packed David and Kristie into the Greenbrier and headed for Ann Arbor. After a wonderful get together with her parents and the Weisses, the Weisses mentioned they were going to Chicago. For some time Sally had been thinking about making a trip to Chicago to see the shop of Seymour the Fox and do some in-person shopping, but she, being directionally impaired, wasn't confident about navigating the trip by herself. But since the Weisses were driving there anyway, they decided Sally should leave the kids with their grandparents and she would just follow the Weisses to Chicago. Once she'd driven the route, she was sure she would be fine on the return trip.

When she got to Seymour's store, she was amazed by the effusively warm welcome she received from Seymour when he heard her name. It was as though he inadvertently thought she was a great celebrity. He invited her to dinner and to see the Movie "Cleopatra" which was just out. She was happy for the invitation, but it all felt strange. Finally she asked as tactfully as she could why she was receiving this welcome. He replied, "Oh, as a single customer, you are my very best. You must be making a lot of money in your business!" She explained that she didn't really have a business and she wasn't making any money at all. He replied, "But it is a business that you do. You must make money. You drive here. You pay freight. You must make money." He explained that she needed to charge a little for each of the services she was providing. So she started charging a little extra, not much, but at least she was no longer losing money. And she was beginning to think about herself and business in a different way.

Sally also remembers the time the kids were supposed to have cleaned up their toys and messes in the basement because the women from Sally's class were going to be working there. When she saw the mess was all still there, she grabbed a broom, not entirely seriously, to make her point. She swung it in their direction, and the broom broke, and they all, including Sally, dissolved in laughter.

Then her horizons expanded again when she wore a beautiful suit she had made to an event at Northern Michigan University in Marquette. The fabric was a wonderful, white, nubbly, woven wool that she'd perhaps purchased in Morocco. She had fashioned a coordinating blouse to go with it and covered her shoes in the same fabric. A man approached Sally and Ward where they were standing and said to Sally, "I understand you made your stunning outfit. May I ask if you would consider teaching?" Ward responded before Sally could, "Well, sure she would." A day or so later a person from the school district contacted her to make the necessary arrangements, and she taught an adult education course called "Something for Nothing." In it she taught how to cover shoes and how to find beautiful fabrics in thrift stores that could be used for creating new and wonderful things. As a result she earned a certification as a teacher in Adult Education.

With four kids already in the school system and seeing an opening on the school board, Sally ran for the open position and won. She clearly represented a way of thinking about schools that was quite unlike what had been the norm in that community. The concept Sally was promoting was called "The Lighted Schoolhouse." She pointed out how the school buildings that sat idle summers, weekends and most evenings could be put to much better use in ways that could benefit the whole community. She suggested different functions that could be performed in the schools, some for which a fee could be charged which would offset the cost of utilities and maintenance. She proposed the huge gym could be used for roller-skating. Users would need to pay a fee to skate that would offset the cost for refinishing the floor at the end of the season. After attending an assembly at which Sally made a speech to the parents about her proposals, Ward said with a chuckle and a shake of his head, "You are absolutely a radical." This was an observation rather than a criticism because any initiative his wife undertook always received his full support.

It was not long after her presentation that Ward got new orders for his next deployment to Greenland, and Sally observed that the voting community was probably greatly relieved not to have to think about Sally's revolutionary ideas for their schools.

31 - Preparing to Put Down Roots

What Sally and Ward hoped and expected would be a temporary calling back into service had turned into a military career that formed the backdrop of their family's lives to date. Though Ward had never planned to be regular military, he thrived in the service. It was standard policy that he would automatically be retired after 20 years of service if he didn't become regular military. He decided that was quite acceptable. He would receive his pension and benefits while still a relatively young man with opportunities to establish a new career in a location of his choice.

With two years before Ward's retirement, the family discussed where they would wish their permanent home to be. Ward and Sally had

Ward at home

enjoyed the mountainous beauty of Colorado when they'd lived there when David and Kristy were tykes. Then at K.I. Sawyer all five kids had fallen in love with skiing and longed to be where they had access to snowy slopes. They decided beautiful Colorado was where they all would choose to be.

The seven Beightols and Kitty the dog set off in the Greenbrier for Colorado to determine where exactly they would build the house that would become their permanent home once Ward finished his last, two, one-year deployments. They found high property with a view of the mountains in a new development in the rolling area of Englewood, now renamed Centennial, outside of Denver proper. The location seemed accessible to wherever Ward was likely to find work professionally. Ward gave Sally the checkbook and said, "Build us a house." Never one to avoid a challenge, she located a place to rent for the family and enrolled the four older kids in the local schools that were known for their quality. With 3 ½ year-old Ralph at home, she planned and worked with builders. She modified available plans, deciding to go down to achieve the needed space on three levels rather than purchasing additional property to build horizontally.

The Denver house on Willow Street

The result was a spacious but also practical house that nestled rather than sprawled. She carefully planned those spaces to meet the needs of her large family. She positioned the house with a large picture window exquisitely framing the mountains to the west and another to catch the sun in the east as it rose to brighten and warm the house in the mornings. The entryway opened to a great floor-to-ceiling mirror that gave the house an expansive and welcoming feeling of airiness and space. She

The mountains

added a lovely fireplace and a spacious kitchen with a perfect space for a large oval table that would became the heart of family activities.

She had handsome industrial strength floor covering flecked with browns and blacks installed throughout the house, the same highly polished flooring one might see in banks or elevators. With Ward away in Greenland, David who was 13 stepped up as the man of the house to help with the heavy work of moving in. With Sally and David working tirelessly together, they were able to schlep in all but the very biggest pieces. In the process, as they sweated and strained near exhaustion, one might catch the eye of the other. And then they would simply dissolve in hysterical laughter. It was a bizarre but permanent bonding between the two that either can evoke even now when they're carrying something together.

So with the heavy lifting done, they looked at the dusty, scuffed, dull-looking, brand new floors. They roused themselves and went back to work and tried their best to clean the floors and make them shine, but everything they tried failed. The floors still looked awful. So Sally grabbed her keys, and she and David jumped in the car and immediately went out and bought an industrial strength floor cleaner with steel wool pads for scrubbing and other soft pads for waxing and buffing. It worked beautifully, and they could nearly see their reflections.

The family was delighted with what would be their nature-filled backyard to the east and the mountain peaks through the picture window to the west. Sally laughs when she recalls little Ralph calling her as he gazed out that window when he was perhaps three and a half: "Mama! Mama, come quick!! Someone stole my mountains!!" when a cloud had slipped down to cover them from view.

The kids anticipated Christmas that first year with a range of emotions. They were excited to be in their new house, but they would be without Ward who was so far away in Greenland where there was only darkness now for months. Sally knew that Ward was hoping for a leave at Christmas, but she said nothing to the kids lest plans change as they so often did with the military. And what a wonderful Christmas present his arrival was for everyone. The kids were ecstatic and so excited to show him through their new home. They still remember with a grin that he turned the wrong way by accident in the entryway and smacked right into the great mirror.

He told the kids that he'd brought the ingredients for "penguin soup" all the way from Greenland. Soup had long been a staple on the Beightol menu since it made good use of leftover cooked vegetables and meats that otherwise might have gone to waste The kids were usually not very excited about having soup; however, when it was penguin soup, well that was altogether different. Far more delicious! Saying goodbye again was difficult, knowing it would be yet another six months until they would be together again.

32 - Greenland

The year that Ward spent in Greenland was a brutal one. The strategic value of the base for deterrence and defense was unquestioned, but its impact on the human spirit and morale was anything but positive. The landscape was barren, desolate and redundant. For months on end the sun barely rose above the horizon. For other months it glared without setting.

Headquarters

Desolate Greenland

The sun barely rises

Ward was Director of Personnel and tasked with the responsibility for maintaining morale and keeping the men in his charge balanced, focused and meaningfully involved in the work of safeguarding the country. But he found it increasingly difficult to do so both for his men and himself. Self-medicating with alcohol seemed to buffer for a while the sense of isolation, sameness and the sense that the world was going on without them.

When Ward returned to Sally and the kids, the debilitating impact of the long year was apparent to Sally. He seemed to have lost his edge.

Ward home for Christmas from Greenland.

33 - One Last Deployment

Ward's next orders would take the Beightols to Hamilton Air Force Base at Bel Marin Keys about an hour north of San Francisco. Sally found renters for their newly completed house in Denver, and they plunged into life 1200 miles west in California. They rented a house on the bay. David loved riding his bike by the ocean, and the word got back to her that when he was out of his mother's range of vision he would put his little brother Ralph on his shoulders and ride with him into the wind. Ralph loved it too, but their growing independence raised Sally's anxiety level, and she "prayed God to help her take care of the kids."

They had a wonderful used sailboat called the Leaky Maru that the daring teenager David loved to take out. If the opportunity arose, he put Ralph on his shoulders again when they sailed into the wind. Sometimes Sally and Ward would take the boat out, and Sally would bring green beans along to "string" to get them ready for dinner when they returned.

Once David took the boat out alone in the bay. The winds came up, and he found himself in serious trouble with the boat capsizing. He somehow at last managed to get himself and the boat safely back to shore.

David remembers that it was in California that he earned his drivers license and loved driving the long, open roads along the coast.

For the Beightols, California was a time for looking at and evaluating possible options since when the year was over, they would at last be free to plot out their own future. They considered the possibility that they might buy the house by the bay, but its $35,000 price tag seemed exorbitant in 1963. Sally now shakes her head at the fact that such houses have price tags in the millions today.

At the base Ward was again the Director of Personnel. In this position he was required to do little flying, but United Airlines approached him hoping to enlist him for a position teaching pilots once he retired. This was another open California option for the Beightols to consider.

Pam, of all the children, had perhaps been the most vulnerable during the family's many moves. California brought Pam her fourth new elementary school in six years. As the next to the last child in a bright, busy family, she rolled with the punches right along with everyone else, but she was at especially vulnerable stages when some of the moves took place. She was six and just being introduced to the fundamentals of reading when the family left Lincoln for Michigan. She did her best to adjust to the new school with its new kids and new curriculum, but there were gaps in her understanding that she didn't know how to fill. She did her best but was devastated by her third grade teacher's scoffing insinuation that Pam was just "dumb." Then the family was off to Denver with yet another new school and another after that in California. She says it was not until she was actually in college that she seriously learned to read. Then she went on, of course, to graduate with honors in her Masters Degree program at Fort Collins.

It was while the Beightols were living in California that Carl Kempainen became a significant presence in their lives It's likely their meeting became a reality because Minnie had stayed in touch with the beloved family who had rescued her from Mrs. Erva when she was 13.

Sally recalls that one winter when she was a youngster her own family went to visit the Kempainens in the Keweenaw. "There were so many boys!" she recalled. Minnie told Sally that when she lived with the family she'd peeled a peck of potatoes for dinner each night. Sally remembers the hole someone cut in the ice in the creek so that everyone could jump into it after super heating in the sauna. Then there was nothing better than drifting off to sleep in the Kempainens' soft featherbeds.

Carl was one of the Kempainen sons who had shooed flies from the cows as a tyke and worked the farm with the family as he grew up. Carl, it turned out, would be in California at the same time that Sally's family would be there. The Beightols and Carl Kempainen hit it off immediately. Carl was now a coffee broker who traveled throughout the world to every place that coffee grows. He was a generous man with a benevolent spirit, a gay man who had achieved great wealth and was not at all showy about his wealth or the worthwhile causes in which he invested his money. Sally found out quite incidentally that he'd paid a musician a year's salary to write a cantata for the Lutheran Church. He sponsored and made possible an assisted living facility in a community where one was needed. And he later went out of his way to benefit the kids of the Beightol family in meaningful ways. Perhaps he felt being a benefactor to Minnie's progeny might help compensate for Minnie's own lost childhood.

Carl Kempainen

34 - "Acres of Golden"

While they were in Denver, Sally decided that since Kitty was such a great dog, she would make a great mother of great pups. Sally played matchmaker with a handsome golden retriever named Blaze of Glory who had won Best of Show in Colorado. By the time they moved to California, Kitty was pregnant when they moved to California where she delivered a litter of adorable pups. As Sally says, "The kids with their pups were "darling, just darling," rolling in the yard with them while trying to remember to watch for tiny piles of poop.

Sally came to know a woman named Mrs. Acres when Sally helped her with decorating questions. In their conversations Sally learned that Mrs. Acres and her husband raised golden retrievers and owned a ranch named "Acres of Golden."

Sally was invited for a visit and found the ranch had a swimming pool just for dogs, a birthing bed for mama dogs in labor, and puppy beds for mamas and their new pups. Visitors could come and visit the ranch, but a curtain would be drawn for privacy if a mama dog was giving birth.

On a shelf behind were dog bones with either pink or blue ribbons. The walls were covered with portraits of dogs, especially noteworthy sires. And the Acres trained dogs and maintained an extensive library of books related to dogs.

Sally was introduced to one of their favorite dog artists and was overwhelmed at the prices people were willing to pay to have the visual reminders of beloved pets adorning their walls.

Sally could see that though the family hated the very thought of parting with the pups, it wasn't feasible for them to have seven dogs. Mrs. Acres opined to Sally that for many people, "Money is no object, but a good dog is." She advised Sally to sell Kitty's pups for not less than $200.00 a piece. This was a good, high price at the time. One lady bought two of the litter; one went to the Seeing Eye Dog School; and the others were placed in loving homes.

By the end of their year in California, they knew that though they had enjoyed their stay, Colorado, not California, was where they truly wanted to be. Ward declined the offer from United Airlines, and they eagerly returned to Colorado.

Karen, Pam, Kris and Ralph with
Kitty's pups

1965...
Sally Finds Her Way Into Business

35 - Starting Anew in Denver

The Beightols were excited to have at last a permanent home. Ward was now free to pursue a civilian career path, something he had been required to put aside when he was "called up" in 1952.

Major Ward Beightol, Air Force retired, was a decorated veteran who had served around the world as a Command Pilot, an interpreter at diplomatic levels, a highly trained military professional trusted with military secrets at the highest level, a proven administrator, an experienced Director of Personnel within the military who also used his educational background in Psychology to benefit young people in the communities in which he lived. Here was Ward - poised to begin his professional life anew.

But the jobs did not present themselves. His excellent resume and qualifications worked against rather than for him. He was perceived as intimidating and over-qualified. His healthy self-esteem that had seemed invincible before Greenland now proved vulnerable. The alcohol that had become a convenient but risky coping mechanism in Greenland became his buffer for the stress and discouragement of being passed over for job after job. Financially things grew increasingly tight as it became apparent that Ward's military pension of $1500 a month was not sufficient to support the family of seven as well as pay their mortgage. Sally was dumbstruck when she discovered that Ward had actually cancelled his life insurance policy to save money. It was time for her to figure out how to augment the family's income.

Her only certification was the one she'd earned in Michigan when she'd briefly taught several courses in adult education. Still, she was able to put it to use to find a job nearby teaching an adult education class that she again entitled, "Something For Nothing." It provided only a modest addition to the family income.

Things seemed to look up when Ward was offered a job as a recruiter for an employment agency, but of Ward's many talents, this was not one of them, and shortly after he was hired, he was fired. He would be another year without work.

36 - Hummels for Karen's Birthday

Sally remembers in detail Karen's 13th birthday, September 29, 1966. It was the first year after Ward's retirement from the Air Force. She remembers it because Karen had her heart set on owning her very

One of Karen's Hummel plaques

One of Karen's birthday Hummels

own Hummel, the charming little German figurines of children. Sally went to a shop where Hummels were sold, but their prices were far more than she could spare. The only Hummels she could afford were merely pictures on little postcards. But Karen would be coming home after school and expecting to see her birthday cake and present on the table. What was she to do? She thought of the decoupage, which was a popular craft at the time, and promptly had an idea! She purchased several of the Hummel postcards and rushed home. She hurried and got the cake baking in the oven and went to look at her millinery supplies. Her Sobo glue would work and the spray for the straw hats would suffice for the multiple layers of polyurethane. Now what to mount them on??? There was a house being built next door where there was a pile of scrap lumber. She searched in the pile and discovered boards that were the perfect size for the six postcards. She used the router to grind the white edges from the mounted postcards. The spray gave the plaques a finished decoupage look. "Wow!" Sally thought, amazed at how quickly and perfectly it had all come about. While they dried, she iced the cake. And by the time Karen got home, the plaques were neatly wrapped beside Karen's birthday cake, and Karen was perfectly delighted with her wonderful birthday gift.

When Sally made the first Hummel plaques for Karen's birthday, Ed was running Win Schuler's, a widely known restaurant with a gift shop in Marshall, Michigan. Sally decided to create a few more of the plaques and send them to her nieces for their birthdays. The girls were delighted, and Ed encouraged Sally to send him some more. He would see if they might sell in the restaurant gift shop. Sally did just that and designed a label with the brand name "Kindercraft" to attach to them, and she sent them off to Ed.

They sold surprisingly well. When the Hallmark representative came in and bought up the entire supply, Ed told Sally she had a winner and should get to work on more before Hallmark got out a product to compete with hers. He advised her to look into getting a patent. Since she couldn't patent the Hummel figures, she decided to try for a patent on the routing technique.

During the years Ed and his family lived in Marshall when Ed was running Win Schuler's, Kristy was a teenager. For a summer job she lived with Ed and his family and waited tables at the restaurant.

Creating Hummels for the gift shop at Win Schuler's was the beginning of a family business that would augment Ward's pension until he became established in a regular civilian job. Sally did the decoupage in the house while Ward did the routing in the garage. Sally said Ward looked like a Hummel himself with sawdust in his hair.

37 - Skiers

The Beightol kids all longed to ski the slopes of Colorado, but skiing was expensive. So during the winter of 1968 Sally got a part time job with the State of Colorado conducting a survey on skis perhaps six to eight times during the ski season. Sally and the other women conducting

the survey would ski up and join people on ski lifts and ask where they preferred to stay, what gas they used, and what kinds of restaurants they preferred. The surveyors were rotated through the various ski resorts of Vail, Aspen, Breckenridge, and

The Skiing Beightols with their Greenbriar: Ralph, David, Kris, Karen Pam, Sally and Ward

Winter Park. For driving to pick up other women conducting the survey, Sally would be paid $5.00. The only other compensations were free skiing the afternoon of the survey and two free additional ski tickets. Her children rotated their turns to use the ski tickets.

Marcie Dillinger was one of the other surveyors, and she always brought tawny port for after skiing. It was just perfect, Sally said, with the peanut butter sandwiches Sally always brought.

Sally notes wryly that it was not on the slopes or getting on or off the lifts that she broke her foot. It was where the surface was perfectly flat and she was not even on survey duty. Carl Kempainen had come to visit them in Colorado, and they'd taken him skiing. As they were heading to the lodge for lunch, Sally's ski caught in a rut and she ended up with her foot in a cast until spring.

38 - A Guardian Angel

When the cast was finally off, Sally was free to concentrate on marketing her Kindercraft items in New York City. Sally needed a place to stay in New York while she was marketing Kindercraft, and the proactive Carl Kempainen stepped in, making arrangements for her to stay right in the middle of Manhattan in the beloved but modest rent-controlled apartment he had maintained there for years. He then got tickets for them to see "Jesus Christ Superstar."

In the years ahead, Carl was to appear again and again as guardian angel for the Beightols. The noted photojournalist for LIFE magazine, Alfred Eisenstaedt, also had an apartment in Carl's building. It was Eisenstaedt who shot the iconic photograph of an ecstatic young sailor giving a surprise kiss to a young woman on hearing that World War II had ended. When David Beightol was pursuing a focus on photography, Carl made it possible for David to go on a photographic expedition as a helper for Alfred Eisenstaedt. And it turned out that

David on location with Alfred Eisenstaedt

Eisenstaedt invited David to share an exhibit with him, meaningfully impacting David's career.And Carl also saw to it that when Ralph, then a young man, was going to visit the New York Stock Exchange, that he was appropriately attired in a Brooks Brothers suit, shirt, tie and shoes so that he looked the part. Carl was there again when Pam's young son Erik was found to need surgery for a tumor behind his eye. And when Kristie was doing her hospital internship in occupational therapy in New York City, Carl contacted her and took her out to dinner.

Carl took it upon himself to be the guardian angel for Minnie's progeny, the guardian angel Minnie had lived without until she was 13.

39 - Marketing the Hummels

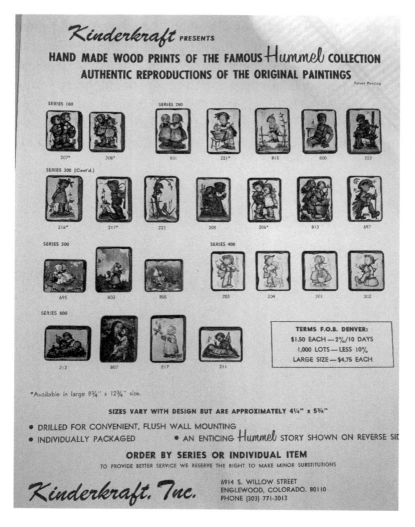

Kindercraft promotional flyer

To promote her Kindercraft plaques In New York, Sally set up appointments with purchasing agents with JC Penney, the May Company and S&H Green Stamps.* The city was hot, Sally said, too hot for her false eyelashes. She decided on a green culottes outfit made of linen with a flat front and back split. Her top was "white with swirls so the sweat marks wouldn't show." To set it off, she had lemon yellow spiked heels. But because her ankle still swelled, she put her yellow shoes in the basket with her Hummel samples and wore an old pair of comfortable sneakers with a hole in the toe between appointments. Then she would find an out of the way spot where she could slip her tennis shoes into her basket and replace them with her yellow pumps for the presentation. Seeing her doing her transformation, one fellow peeked in and asked her with charmed curiosity, "Please tell me what you're selling."

She was delighted when she got her first moderate orders for the plaques. Surprisingly, though, it was on the reorders that thousands more were placed. The orders became too much for the garage, and they rented another space to use for the woodworking shop. They thought about buying the property for $20,000, but it seemed awfully expensive. It would end up the property for which Target paid truly big bucks to erect a new store.

They actually earned between one and two thousand dollars a month for nearly three years selling Kindercraft. Sally's best friend from high school, Gerry Hepner, was married to a fellow who was a representative for many products and arranged for Kindercraft to be sold at military Base Exchanges. And to think it was all a result of Sally's desperate idea for a gift for Karen's birthday. Eventually their patent was denied, but in the interim, the business did very well.

*S&H Green Stamps was a popular rewards program for shoppers. Many many businesses distributed stamps at checkout based on the dollar value of the purchase. Then customers licked the stamps and saved them in special booklets S&H provided. A filled booklet equaled 1200 points that could be spent on a vast number of items from the S&H catalogue

40 - Up Troublesome Creek Road

A neighbor on Willow Street told Sally about a wonderful place for them to investigate, knowing the Beightols loved to go out exploring in the extraordinary state they had chosen to be their new home. She gave them directions that led up Troublesome Creek Road to beautiful, wild property on a hill atop a mountain. The area was known as Big Horn Park. The ruggedness of the place, out among the mountain peaks and under the open sky, moon, and stars exhilarated them. They instantly decided to see if they could purchase land there and negotiated the deal in the nearest town called Kremling. There they also found a motel where they could stay called the "Hoof and Horn Motel."

The year they purchased the property they made it the destination for their August 6th Celebration. The date always marked a great day of festivity in the Beightol family because it was the day Willis flew in to pin Ward's pilot wings on his chest, the day WW II ended in Europe, and the day Ward and Sally got married. And that year it also turned out to be the date of the full moon.

Kristy had driven up to meet them in the old Mercedes Ward had bought for her that they'd named "The Professor." She brought a bottle of champagne, and they toasted the new adventure under the full moon and then wedged the bottle in a tree to commemorate the auspicious event. The next year they found that bears had shredded the tree all around the bottle, marking it in an even more emphatic way. That first evening they built a bonfire and sang and reveled under a moon so big and bright that they could read beneath it. After that they loved whenever they could be there to celebrate August 6th, and were delighted that it so often arrived with a full moon.

If the roads weren't too slushy or treacherous, the family would all go up the mountain in the Winnebago they'd bought from Aunt Elma and Uncle Don.

The family shared their enthusiasm about their find, and soon Carl Kempainen and other friends also bought property in Big Horn Park. There was in the area a very old, abandoned cabin once used by

Enjoying Big Horn Camp with friends

hunters. It had framed bunks, and people who had property in the area shared in its use. The Beightols often enjoyed it, and Sally even made curtains for it.

Near the cabin was a platform once used by hunters for setting up their tents. It was covered with tarpaper. The Beightols and their friends took off the tarpaper, removed the nails, sanded the splinters and made it into a dance floor. Sally remembers the time David and his friends brought a generator and speakers. Then they posted signs inviting anyone who wished to to come, and there were 50 people who enjoyed the event.

The dance floor beside the cabin

The next morning the 15 or 20 people who were still there had had pancakes outside for breakfast. They decided to do a meditation tape that one had brought and were all lying prone on the platform when a car drove up. Not knowing what to make of the prone bodies, the car turned around and went back down the mountain, a cause for much theorizing and laughter afterwards.

David made this wonderful place the location of his wedding in 1976, and he composed a special song for the event. The festivities were held at an airy and beautiful home that had just been completed nearby. Then they all danced on the platform and set sawhorses on it for food.

Ward and Sally sometimes just enjoyed getting away to camp, especially with their friends, the Jensens. The Jensens owned a regular tent, but Ward and Sally had acquired a formerly owned tent that they could put atop their car to keep them up and safe from the critters on the ground. They had fun with it until one day a wind caught it in traffic, tore it from the roof.

The car tent

41 - An Actual Job

Since Sally had experienced her first surprising success with the Kindercraft business, and since Ward's work was inconsistent, Sally was on the lookout for other possible means of augmenting their income. It was 1970 when she answered an ad in the paper for persons with adult education certification and an art background. She sent her resume to the address in Chicago that turned out to be the national headquarters for the Montgomery Ward Company. They were hiring for positions having to do with home decorating. Sally knew nothing about decorating, but she eagerly studied the book she was given.

She was hired along with two other fellows to teach home decorating in Montgomery Ward stores. The corporate theory was that if someone who had nothing to do with business taught a course in their store, it could actually serve to increase sales and encourage people to open charge accounts. Research had indicated that people with credit cards spent 30% more than those without, so Sally was given credit card applications that she could distribute.

The two men were each given one store, and Sally was given two, meaning she had twice the responsibility and taught twice the number of classes. An additional responsibility was to create around the store's edges three vignettes or small model room displays that showed the store's furnishings off to great advantage and helped people envision what they might be able to do with their own homes. So Sally was responsible for not three but six vignettes. She rose to the occasion with great success and had been doing so for about a year and a half when one day she and her two colleagues were talking about salary. This was a subject she had been cautioned not to raise because she had been told she was actually making more money than her colleagues. To her dismay she discovered they were in fact making twice as much as she was for half the work, and she was proving herself vastly more successful than either of them. She was furious and pleaded the injustice of her case to corporate headquarters in Chicago, but they were adamant about what they were willing to pay a woman, so Sally quit.

But the managers of both stores where she worked were eager to hire her. She chose the 84th Street store, and wanting to come across as a confident, experienced professional, she informed the interviewer that she preferred to work on straight commission of 6%, not on salary. The interviewer said that wouldn't be possible because the company's policy was that everyone worked on 6% commission if they met or exceeded quota, but if they fell below it they received a standard minimum. Sally was sure she wasn't going to fall below quota, and she never did. She was placed in the furniture department where she also met John Bagwell, a wonderful draperies installer who became her mentor and taught her all she needed to know about the world of draperies.

42 - 1 % Commission and Mr. Maroon

One day a notice from headquarters circulated through the store stating that if an employee sold a commercial contract, the employee would be entitled to a 1% commission on the entire sale. Most just discarded the notice, but Sally realized that this could be a significant opportunity to make money. When that afternoon she walked out the back door of the store, what she saw taking place on the land behind the store registered in a new way in her brain. A builder was creating what looked like a whole city of new homes there. Sally made her way through the construction site to the construction trailer where she introduced herself to a man she learned was the builder, Fred Sprowl. Their conversation segued to an invitation from Fred for Sally to decorate three model homes for him, and soon a contract was drawn up between the builder and Montgomery Ward. The purchase price of Sprowl's new homes would include carpet, and the customers would come to the Montgomery Ward store to pick out and perhaps upgrade their carpet. This would give Sally an opportunity to sell them at retail prices furniture, draperies, a mattress or whatever else they needed for their new homes.

Montgomery Ward headquarters sent a man named Ed Maroon to manage the carpet sales with the builder. Ed Maroon actually wore maroon suits, and Sally notes, his shoulders always carried a sprinkling of dandruff. Sally wished she could have heard the negotiations between Fred Sprowl and Ed Maroon before Maroon came with semi trucks filled with carpets. Sally began to realize that the carpet Maroon was delivering was of reduced fiber content and poorer quality than what he was being paid to deliver. He was remarkably casual about his record keeping, telling Sally to simply send all the paperwork to an address in Chicago. Ward cautioned Sally to keep copies of everything, and she did. Eventually it became apparent to the store manager, Mr. Cox, that neither Sally nor Fred Sprowl nor the store were getting credit for the sales that were being made. Sally eventually would receive only very small portions of what she was entitled to, and Mr. Cox and others began to surmise about methods Maroon must be using to divert money. But the matter did not go to court, and Montgomery Ward lost the contract with Fred Sprowl.

43 - "Inter-selling"

     With the commercial contract lost, Sally went back to selling furniture and draperies in the furniture department. When customers wanted drapes, Sally would make appointments with them to go to their homes with samples to take measurements. Sometimes people also wished advice as to what to do with their homes that would meet their needs and be both affordable and attractive. Sally would then arrange for visits to their homes to figure things out together with them. One of Sally's customers wrote the following letter of appreciation for her visit:

Mrs. Sally Beightol   April 5, 1973
Denver (North Valley)

It happened, a great commotion arose in the front room of our new house. My wife seemed so solid in her views for decorating the house. I the man-mouse had some misgivings as to her certainties. What to do?
We called Montgomery Wards and were introduced to Sally –
Now, Sally is an aggressive, intelligent lady-woman that you know will interject some readjustments. Sally flashes a nice gingival line, and you are reminded of a saying – "walk slowly as you pass through this field of flowers." Her inner gaiety is so easily surfaced.

My wife and I drove Sally up in the hills to our new house –later be our new home. It was impossible to reach the house by car, for a light snow had stalled the car a half mile from the naked house that needed carpeting, drapes, refrigerator and stove.

This inner gaiety came through so naturally – on with the boots and "Let us tramp the rest of the way and see what we shall see." This tenacity to help, and I suspect, pride in her professional skill was so delightful.. Sally is not one to orient your house to show her high fashion, but positive suggestions are advanced to elicit you personality as to color, texture and taste. The lady Sally is a person so sure of herself, in her skill, that she has at her command the power of gentleness combined with the strength of patience.

Walking that day on the slippery road to our house, Sally led all the way. I was reminded of a line, "Oh what fun it is to ride in a one horse open sleigh."

She has mastered the art of unselfish listening. I'm sure her children call her blessed. (Modern translation for "blessed," –"Hi, Mom.")

                                    John Harold

As time went on she suggested other items from other departments of the store that customers might purchase to enhance their homes – stoves, refrigerators, TVs and whatever. Sally earned commissions on these sales as well as ones from her own department, and she did amazingly well, actually being recognized by Montgomery Ward as its "Best Independent Sales Person in the Nation." She had reached this pinnacle because she had made herself knowledgeable about what other products her customers might want that were found in other departments of the store. This led to a dispute between different store managers who felt that "inter-selling" between departments as Sally had done ought not to be allowed because salespeople considered departments exclusively their own.

Mr. Cox, Sally's manager, was delighted with her success and wanted to empower others to do what Sally was doing. He approved Sally's hiring of six new designers.

Sally and the other designers were to go to various luncheons and events to speak about decorating. Each was responsible for creating a presentation. Sally's was entitled "How to Make Your Home Look Like Money is No Object on a Budget You Can Afford." The designers encouraged their audience members to also come to the store and ask for the designer by name. The approach was a great success, and in three months, sales leaped 10%.

But it was a major change to the way selling had always been done at Montgomery Ward. Everybody who wasn't doing it hated it. Then one day word came from headquarters that those new hires were to be placed in departments, and "Don't let them inter-sell!" Sally was so frustrated that she sighed, threw up her hands and laughed, "So long. I quit. It was fun while it lasted.'

Mr. Cox said, "Don't quit. What about becoming a manager?" This drew Sally's attention, and she thought, "Well, maybe." What he proposed was that she be a manager of a "seconds center" warehouse of items that had been rejected for a variety of reasons. She and Mr. Cox agreed that it would be a good place for her to expand her range of skills, and they came to terms on what her contract would be and what she would be paid. And then she got the letter from headquarters saying, "We will have no women as managers." The letter also pointed out that the warehouse Sally would have run had no air conditioning, and it questioned how in the world a woman could "get the pool tables set up." This time there was no doubt that her quitting was final.

It is difficult for us to promote this program because we have to rely on a local newspaper with very limited circulation.

Ideally this program should be set up in a central location for the entire District with a full scale advertising program, using TV and newspaper stating we have 20 qualified decorators that will help with any and all decorating problems. The sales would be credited to the stores by postal zones.

I am also attaching a copy of an ad Sears ran November 22, selling a "Total Concept" in contract sales. I think we should go both directions tying in home sales and contract sales.

Again, the success will only come through hiring professional salespeople. Our Department Manager, Sally Beightel is this kind of professional. If she has an 8:00 A.M. or 10:00 P.M. appointment, she makes them cheerfully. She is interested in sales and one of her best source for prospects is making talks on Home Decorating to any club or group that she can. Her only fee is the names and addresses of the members present.

We are keeping accurate records on this program and will keep you posted.

H. C. Cox

44 - Willow Street, This Time in Denver

The kids were now growing up on Willow Street in Denver just as their mother had done on Willow Street in Ann Arbor. During the years until the role of primary breadwinner shifted from Ward to Sally, the family had moved so many times that the kids automatically relied on their mother and siblings as a team of constants when their playmates, friends, and associates came and went with each move. Their father fortified the team whenever he was there, but he was often away at work. Sally and Ward explained to the kids that each child needed to help them watch out for and help take care of the next younger one.

Pam remembers how odd it felt when her mom who had always been such a permanent presence at home was now also away at work. Pam was in junior high and expected to be responsible for Ralph after school. The older kids were in high school, and Ralph was in elementary school.

But Sally was still an active participant in the activities of the family. Sally's lifelong love of sewing began as a child when she and her mother learned to sew together. In Denver she realized that with three teenage daughters, it was time they learned to love it and its powers well. She scouted out a sewing

machine for each of the girls and set them all up on the lower level of the Denver house as a classroom. They all learned a skill for their lifetimes too.

Sally sewing in Alaska with Karen

In the military, the kids were used to simple, generic church services, but the Lutheran church services in Denver involved all kinds of ups and downs, and the services were long. So they went across the street to check out the Methodist church. There they found a minister they liked and services that were direct and much briefer.

Sally became the sponsor of the church's youth group. They planned a skiing outing, and the response was so enthusiastic that two busloads signed up. Sally needed someone else to go along to help chaperone. A fellow named Chuck Shobender volunteered to help, and Sally asked if he could ski, implying she wasn't interested in a mere observer. He confirmed that he could, and she welcomed him to join her. They loaded the kids onto the buses, and when Chuck put on his jacket Sally saw it bore the insignia of the national director of the ski patrol. They spent the morning monitoring the kids, and he asked if she wanted to take a ski at lunch. He led her to the Black Diamond, the most demanding course, assuming she could ski. He was a beautiful skier. He flew, but they had to roll Sally down. Nevertheless, they became fine friends.

The family attended a magic show at Ralph's elementary school where the magician did a trick that involved a rabbit. He asked the audience if anyone would like to have the rabbit to take home with them. Little Ralph's enthusiastic hand shot up in an instant as he shouted, "I would!" The magician spotted his eager face first, and the Beightols acquired a new family member, Rabbit Rabbit. Rabbit Rabbit not only got along beautifully with Kitty, but also went very nicely on walks with his own collar and leash.

And for a year, the family expanded again when Annelise, an exchange student from Switzerland, came to live with them.

Her parents came for a visit, and Ward and Sally were able to travel with them and introduce them to the wonders and places of interest in the western United States. They visited Las Vegas, Nevada, known for its gambling and entertainment. There they came upon the statue of a Roman gladiator with his arm raised aloft. One of the group proposed that Sally go and pose with it for a picture.

Ward and Sally with Annelise, Pam, Kris Karen, David and
Ralph with Kitty

She obliged and impishly threw her hand up as the counterpart
female gladiator. That moment frozen in history is the cover of this
book.

The firm relationship between families continued when Kristy
went abroad to live with Annelise and her family in Switzerland. And
later still, Sally, Kris and her daughter Kate went to visit the family after
a trip to Paris.

45 - Ralph, Ed and the Challenge of Dyslexia

Ralph was everyone's little brother. He grew up a vital, active boy with a compassionate heart and inquisitive mind. He loved to ski, fix other kids' bikes and just fix stuff in general. Sally would bring home broken equipment that had been discarded, and Ralph would love trying to figure out what the problem was and trying to get it back working again.

Ralph, like Sally's brother Ed, was dyslexic, a hereditary condition. Because of a quirky "slipped synapse" in the minute space where the visual input of letters connects to receivers in the brain that reproduce them in sensible and predictable patterns, a dyslexic person sees a complicated jumble. Imagine looking through glasses that reversed or misaligned or scattered the letters that formed messages in front of you. Despite the intelligence and will of people with dyslexia, efficiently extricating meaning from the jumble can be impossible. Little was known of dyslexia when Ed was a child, and people assumed he either wasn't trying hard enough and/or he just wasn't very bright. Neither was true, but he was made to feel guilty and inadequate because of his difficulty reading. Sally and the Beightol family were determined that Ralph's life would not be tainted by this one irregularity. His sisters stepped in and read and read to him, enriching and informing him about fields of knowledge and enjoyment that he might be cut off from otherwise. Karen who went on to be a teacher, principal and school superintendent, made it her responsibility to help him learn to read. And Ralph, like his uncle Ed, learned to compensate and graduated from college.

46 - Possibly Antiques?

Sally had aggressively plunged into the world of work at Montgomery Ward, learning so much and gaining so much experience that by the time she separated from the company she felt primed to tackle a new business challenge.

She was open to options when she met Virginia Lillard while playing bridge. Virginia was an antiques dealer who owned three antique stores, one a barn with quarters above where she lived. She told Sally she was considering taking on an administrative assistant who might assume responsibility for running the business when she was ready to retire. Was Sally interested?

Sally said she knew nothing about antiques, but Virginia insisted she would teach her what she needed to know and invited Sally and Ward to accompany her on an antiques buying trip to Vienna and Paris. Would they come?

"Well, sure, yes," and they happily took her up on the offer. Ward was particularly excited at the prospect of returning to Paris where he'd spent such unforgetable time as a young Air Force pilot during the war. And then he was ecstatic when he learned that Virginia had ordered tickets for the opera in Vienna.

Sally accompanied Virginia, observing and learning, as she bought thousands of dollars worth of antiques, "a boatload?" But it was terribly disappointing that Virginia seemed to have no interest in savoring their time abroad in the way Ward and Sally had hoped to. And when it turned out that the opera tickets Virginia had purchased had been for the day before, not the day they actually went to the opera house, the music-loving Ward was devastated. "We were right here, and we could have gone!" He lamented.

On their return to Denver, Sally took on responsibilities as Virginia delegated them to her. Sally made a sizable sale of antiques to the Spaghetti Factory – a chain that charmingly decorated its restaurants with antiques of all kinds.

Virginia asked Sally to take over the the task of arranging the working hours for the employees, but then Virginia invariably quibbled with Sally about the details.

Sally realized Virginia had no real system of money management or bookkeeping. She kept money and receipts randomly stuffed into bags here and there. But when Sally made suggestions about organizing a system, Virginia was defensive and combative. It was increasingly clear that the two were not going to be able to work in a professional relationship. Sally couldn't do things Virginia's way, and Virginia wasn't going to change. She smiled at Virginia one day as she asked her, "You don't really want to quit and retire, do you?" And Virginia admitted that perhaps she didn't. They parted professional company but remained friends.

47 - Time For a Business of Her Own

Then the risk-taker in Sally felt it was time for her to try her hand at a business of her own. She had learned a great deal in the time she had been with Montgomery Ward and decided to take what she had learned and put it to use in her own enterprise. She found office space on Yosemite, a thoroughfare within walking distance of the Willow Street house, and she named the business "Final Touch." Her concept was to create an appealing studio where customers could come in to select carpets, draperies, window shades and wallpaper for their homes. She would also help them as a professional decorator to shop and select the other items that would give the final touch of perfection to their homes. Designers nearby would also come to Sally's shop to place orders. She sold carpet, draperies, window shades and wallpaper and boasted a superb "workroom" of excellent professionals for installing carpet, hanging wallpaper, making and installing drapes and shades as well as upholsterers and seamstresses. "Perfection and Good Business" was her motto.

The seamstress who produced perfection for her, the best she had ever encountered, was a World War II war bride who had been raised attending Nazi kids' camps. "She was," Sally says, "a Nazi to the bone. but a magnificent seamstress." She taught her husband, Bernard Carlucci who was a cook by trade, how to do hems to hide the threads. The quality of the couple's work was unequaled anywhere. The woman posed the eternal ethical question of how to deal with the presence of both the magnificent and the awful in the same person. Sally decided to do her best to provide her customers the perfection and good business practices she promised while trying to deftly sidestep the woman's painful flaw. Sally and the business prospered until the economy began its slide into recession.

48 - Ward Refocuses

Ward fortunately landed a fine job as purchasing agent for American Snow Blast, a firm that made machinery for removing snow from runways at airports throughout the country. He would remain with the company until nearly all of the kids were out of college.

At first, though, Ward got in the habit of stopping after work with the guys from Snow Blast for a drink or two or five. He was instinctively at home in male company. He had grown up with four brothers. At Michigan State studying Psychology he focused on assisting young men who had gotten caught up in the legal system. He had grown up without a father to mentor him and was always drawn to opportunities where he could help young men succeed. In Lincoln he'd been recognized for the instrumental role he played in creating procedures for the juvenile courts of Nebraska. Then serving as Director of Personnel in various deployments, he worked directly with young men. In the Air Force his colleagues were almost exclusively male. So "after working hours" camaraderie felt like a relaxed extension of that familiarity. But his time in Greenland had established alcohol as essential to achieving his sense of relaxation and wellbeing. Now Ward was regularly late getting home, causing Sally to worry, knowing that he would be driving home while almost certainly impaired.

The issue came to a head August 6th. The date August 6th was always a day of celebration for the Beightols because it marked three enormously significant events: the day he received his pilot's wings; the day the armistice ended WW II, and the day Ward and Sally were married. This August 6th was their 25th wedding anniversary, and she was anticipating his arrival home, knowing they would absolutely be doing special things to honor it that evening. But Ward got caught up at the bar and forgot. He rolled in far too late and in no condition to honor the day of all days. It was for Sally clearly the last straw. He would have to straighten up or move out. To his credit, he reeled it back in and kept it under control.

Ward clearly needed some primarily male activity in his life that was compelling, enjoyable, social, and truly utilized his talents. He found it with "The Society for the Preservation and Encouragement of Barbershop Singing in America." He loved it!

The actual origins of Barbershop singing are a bit foggy. People have theorized that barbers in England in the mid 19th century may have begun humming or singing while they tended to their customers, and those sitting in the shops may have joined in, and it gradually caught on. This can't be documented, but Barbershop's roots in the Black musical heritage of America can. Certain elements can be traced to field singing, blues, ragtime and jazz. Between Vaudeville acts while scenes were being changed, quartets, usually Black, would come out in front of the curtain to entertain the audience singing a cappella. They dressed in colorful costumes to be visible to those in the less expensive seats. In each quartet there was "the second tenor" who carried the melody, "the first tenor" who sang harmony above him, "the bass" who provided the foundation, and "the baritone" who filled in the middle spaces.

Ward's Barbershop quartet was named "The Amazing Grays," and the hymn "Amazing Grace" was their signature song. Ward sang bass. "The Amazing Grays" were indeed amazing grace for Ward and Sally. Being involved in barbershopping provided him a creative outlet for his passion for music and brought him the satisfaction of collaborating closely with other men, young and old, to bring delight to others' ears. The men would meet every Monday night to practice.

Amazing Grays — 1989
Ward Beightol, Gene Carrier, Pete Donohue, Harlan Fletcher

The Amazing Grays

While they did, Sally would play bridge with Alice Hulings, the wife of another barber shopper, and two of Alice's friends. Margie was a fellow music teacher with Alice in the public schools and the other friend was Rosamund Godwin Austin who proudly went by her full name. They called themselves "The Golden Girls" and became great friends. They played so often that once they played four games without realizing they were missing four cards.

Every 4th of July for 20 years Ward, his barbershopper friends and their wives traveled to various cities to participate in

The Golden Girls

an international barber shoppers event with other quartets from the country and beyond. They referred to it informally as "The Chorus." The women traveled, shopped, and thoroughly enjoyed for years the time they spent together. Ward's other saving grace was the garden that he grew in the backyard. He was happily content to work there by the hour. Often he wore earphones and would be practicing his bass parts for the quartet. Ward could hear their voices in his earphones, but all the family could hear would be Ward singing his bass parts, and it always made them laugh.

49 - Fred's Health

In the meantime, Sally got a call from her mother saying that while she and Sally's father were on vacation, he had been taken to the hospital. Fred was a gregarious salesman who bloomed in social settings and enjoyed alcohol for its role in easing interactions and taking the edge off the stresses of life. For many years he seemed to handle it well, only very rarely overindulging. But over that time he became increasingly dependent upon it, relying on it to keep him at a level where he felt he performed optimally. He would start the day with a shot in the morning "to get the juices flowing," he'd say with the shake of his head and a "Brrrr." Then throughout the day he kept himself "on maintenance" with booster shots. At the hospital the doctor told Minnie there was no doubt that her husband was an alcoholic. Minnie said she was certainly aware that her husband drank, but she said she didn't consider him an alcoholic, "He never hit me," she told the doctor.

After the diagnosis, Minnie pleaded and pleaded with Fred to just "stop drinking," but by then he couldn't. He grew increasingly despondent after suffering what Sally thinks must have been a stroke. He had difficulty walking and was sent to rehabilitation. While they walked there, Sally remembers her dad, a man who adored the thrill of powerboat racing and who had spent his entire professional life on the road, saying, "Oh my God, the cars! They scare me! I can't watch." Minnie surrounded him with things he'd always enjoyed and checked out new books from the library that she thought would interest him, but he was depressed, ill and nothing seemed to make a difference.

One day he made arrangements with a garage to get their car serviced. Minnie took the car but discovered at the garage that the appointment was not for that day but the next. So she returned home earlier than expected to find her husband in the bathtub, having saved up all his meds and taken them all at once in an effort to kill himself. The ambulance came, and though he did survive, he never really did recover. Arrangements were made for him to have nursing home care, but once there, he wouldn't eat. He wouldn't try. He wanted death and finally achieved it. It was July 7th, 1977. He was 71.

Karen was in Maine working as a summer camp counselor when she got the call that her grandfather had died. She immediately headed for Ann Arbor and Minnie. Minnie's friend Esther took Minnie to the airport to pick up Sally when her late evening flight came in, but they couldn't find her and assumed she must have missed her flight. So they went back home without finding Sally who was there at the airport hunting for them. Sally found a limo going to one of the Ann Arbor hotels, and when she got there, the driver insisted on driving her the rest of the way home.

Sally remembers writing and delivering the eulogy for her father's funeral service:

July 7, 1977

"I'd like to share some thoughts of and about my father –
The first recollection of the man I called "Daddy" was in connection with the acrid smell of burning fuel, the intense notice of racing motor boats, Mother's excitement and my identity with the man out there competing. I was much too young to know at that time how Dad's attitude toward competition and winning would influence all those around him, plus, make firm in my mind that the difference between first and second place was just that little extra effort.

Dad's attitude and influence were witnessed again when I watched him play volley ball – and be of course made All American. I watched him take bad situations and turn them to the advantage and good. Dad was a real salesman! His salesmanship was not only used in his profession but in doing good works. The Trinity Lutheran Church structure is a monument to his talent.

This big guy liked to give the façade of being gruff and tough, but he was really a loving and sensitive person. (He was very careful though to make sure no one was looking.)

I remember bringing home the first Grandbaby and watching that big man with the big hands trying to figure out how to hold him – I still chuckle. My David and "Boom-Pa" as he called him had many fun times together fishing and learning together. "Boom-Pa" was a neat Grandpa.

In this day of child rearing books and volumes of words on the subject, I've thought of how few words and actions my father used.

For instance – as a teenager trying to sneak in after hours, I can still hear from his bedroom, "nothing good happens after midnight" (You know he was right).

Other sayings, not terribly profound but always in my mind –

"You can drive my car when you can afford to buy one."

"Help your mother."

"How can you look like you stepped out of a bandbox and leave your room such a mess?"

"Clean your plate."

"Help me put up the flag."

"Too much make up."

"You will too go to Sunday School"

"No you can't get married, go to College (I went in the fall).

There was no question in our house about right and wrong, no grey areas, just black and white. What an easy way to establish values. For this I thank my Dad and my children thank him.

My father didn't collect things, he collected people, he was a leader who loved an active life, loved good food, drink and good times. But most of all he loved my mother, his home and family. When Dad was well, he didn't waste a minute of his life, he enjoyed the challenges and the pleasures, he enjoyed and loved his friends and relatives = you people that are here today. So rejoice with us today that my father is enjoying his new adventure – the challenges and pleasures of a new life.

Mother, Eddy and I are glad you are with us. My father loved you –

Minnie remained on Willow Street in Ann Arbor for two more years. She did her best to resume her life with the church, friends and bridge. One day she got a call from Sally saying that the little house across the street from the Beightol house in Denver was for sale. It was a perfect opportunity. Would she come? Minnie decided she would.

Pam and John were newlyweds at that time in 1979 and went to Ann Arbor to help Minnie organize, pack, disperse or sell all that the house had accumulated over half a century. Then Sally helped put the

Pam in Sally's gown

house on the market. Soon two lawyers were delighted to purchase it and poured their hearts into beautifully renovating it. In the meantime, John who was a builder renovated Minnie's new home on Willow Street in Denver for her and even installed a fireplace.

And not long after that, Kris and Jimmy Mawhinney also married.

Kris in Sally's gown

50 - Spirit Lake

But in the meantime in Denver, Sally moved Final Touch to a new location that she thought would be more conducive to business, but given the faltering economy, business continued to be slow.

One day a young customer of hers from Iowa came into Final Touch to select carpet. He loved Sally's concept of having such a wonderful little place to pick out things. When his dad, Wayne Crim, came into town, his son took him to Sally's store as well. The dad was taken with the store, with Sally, and with her skills. He asked her if she could consider coming to Iowa to manage the furniture store he had recently purchased, Tonsfeldts in Spirit Lake, Iowa near fashionable Lake Okoboji. He was a freewheeling and successful farmer who had purchased Tonsfeldts, a high-end furniture and decorating store, from its founders. Wayne Crim was a farmer, not a decorator, and now he was in the market for the perfect knowledgeable person to run it and be its public face. Sally could see that the immediate prospects for Final Touch in Denver were much less promising than the farmer's offer at Tonsfeldts in Iowa, and after talking it over with Ward, decided, "Well, sure." They would give it a try. Sally would sign a contract for two years to help the farmer achieve success in his new business. Ward was now retired and not tied to a location. And Minnie was ready for something new too. They could sell Final Touch, rent the houses, and play the next two years by ear.

So Sally needed to sell or close Final Touch. Closing it was a problem because she had signed a contract to rent the current space and would still be obliged to honor the rental agreement if she closed the business. So she put the business on the market, but the economy was still sluggish and she got no promising offers. Having obligated herself to be at work at Spirit Lake, she left Ward in Denver to mind the business and take care of the installations she had already committed to.

Wayne Crim told Sally he would be happy to fly her to Iowa in his plane, and she happily accepted. His plane was even at Arapaho Airport near her home. But when she got to the airport, she was dismayed that the plane seemed to be a crop-duster, and she was "a nervous wreck" all the way to Iowa.

Notice in the paper of Sally's joining
Tonsfeldt

She was pleased to find that Spirit Lake was indeed a nice little town where wealthy people from lake Okoboji came to shop. Tonsfeldts had been a stable feature of the town for decades, the shop where wealthy clients from Lake Okoboji came to buy their furniture. The store had been created by Ada Tonsfeldt, a decorator who had owned and run it until deciding to put it up for sale. Wayne Crim and this new manager represented such a dramatic change of course that some of the employees who had been with the store for 30 or more years were aloof and skeptical. Sally thought the reaction was to be expected and came prepared to prove herself.

Wayne Crim made temporary arrangements for Sally to be put up in a beautiful place on Lake Okoboji that was for sale and being shown. One night she couldn't sleep. The night was calm and beautiful, and she walked the docks. Tonsfeldts wasn't what was bothering her. What was keeping her awake was what she was going to do about Final Touch in Denver. As she walked she thought and prayed for help to figure out what her next step should be,

So Sally was stunned when the very next day a couple came into Tonsfeldts and said they had decided to buy her Denver store. She was speechless with gratitude for what seemed nothing short of a miracle. The transaction went smoothly, Final Touch gained new owners, and Ward and Minnie came to Spirit Lake to join Sally.

Spirit Lake house

Ward was enthusiastic about the prospect of being in Iowa not too far from his brother Bob and close to where he'd grown up. Minnie too was ready for a new adventure. They found a very nice place to rent that was the first house to be built in a new development. The development had an in-ground swimming pool, tennis courts and other convenient amenities. All of these they had completely to themselves because no other houses were constructed the whole time they lived there because of the downturn in the economy. Ward inquired if there were restrictions about putting in a garden. Finding there were none, he quickly got to work tilling and planting. The garden was wonderfully productive, and Sally and Minnie had fun planning meals around what they harvested. Someone asked Ward what he did when

158

Ward the gardener

Pheasants shot by Ward and his
brother Bob

animals, especially raccoons, ate his corn. He said, "Oh, I just plant two more rows of corn." Ward loved the experience of hunting again with his brother Bob. They brought home so many pheasants and found they were delicious with sauerkraut.

Wayne Crim was another business person not unlike Virginia Lillard who seemed to have no inclination to keep organized books or records. Wayne Crim, however, was even more extreme than Virginia Lillard. He might trade hay or his wife's clothing for furniture. Sally was thankful not to have to deal with the bookkeeping at Tonsfeldts. This job was the responsibility of Betsy Holzhauer who rolled her eyes when Wayne Crim would present her with another unorthodox financial transaction that she would have to figure out how to record.

It was Betsy Flint Holzhauer who played matchmaker with her father Frank Flint, the son of a minister, and Sally's mother Minnie Meyer. They both had had spouses for many years whom they'd lost. Fred had died four years earlier. Frank and Minnie found they enjoyed each other's company and especially enjoyed playing cribbage and euchre together. The idea of marrying just felt right, and the family came to celebrate their wedding that was held in the Episcopal Church in Spirit Lake. The newlyweds found a cute house there in town.

Looking back on their two years at Spirit Lake, Sally says, "Everyone had a great time!"

51 - The Cayman Islands

Betty Munson was one of Sally's customers at Tonsfeldts, and Betty was the reason Sally discovered the Cayman Islands. Betty was a nurse who had been married to her husband Harry for many years. He was a farmer, and since farming can be precarious financially, Betty had kept a close eye on the balance in the checkbook. They were making ends meet, but just barely. So the two lived an absolutely no-frills, exceedingly frugal life for decades. They worked all the time, and still Betty combed the second-hand stores for their clothes and furnishings. They cut corners wherever they could and drove old Chevys.

Then one day Harry became very ill and revealed that he actually had another bank account. Betty at first could not grasp the magnitude of what he had done. And then when she did, she pivoted her energy, as if it were a laser, away from austerity and aimed it at all the wishes and dreams she had long suppressed. There was money for everything, and she was going to use it. She built a glass-enclosed year-around swimming pool at the farm. She bought a Cadillac, and she bought a wonderful place in the Cayman Islands. At first her husband howled at his wife's extravagances, but then he found he was quite okay with them, saying she actually should have bought two places. Ward remembered, however, going

The Munsons, Betty and Harry

with him in an old broken down wreck of a car to a repair shop where he then tried to finagle and whittle down the mechanic's reasonable price for an old used tire. And for frugal Ward to take exception to this, it had to be clearly way over the top.

Sally and Ward in the Caymans

Betty invited Sally and Ward to come to the Caymans, which they did, renting the second floor of the Munsons' large home. Ward and Sally returned each year for six years and stayed two or three weeks, often bringing friends. Twenty-five years after Ward and their friends in Morocco had their picture taken at the bullfights in Spain, the same group met again in the Caymans and posed for an identical photograph.

David brought his family to the Caymans, and they rented the basement level of the Munson house. They loved the short walk to the beach where they could swim to a sunken ship among hundreds of little fish. When Ralph graduated from college he also enjoyed a month in this tropical haven.

52 - Miss Lassie

It was on the Beightols' first trip to the Caymans that Betty and Sally were walking into town when a small cottage caught Sally's eye because of the intriguing and colorful scenes and figures that were painted on its shutters. So on their way back from town, to satisfy Sally's curiosity, they stopped and knocked. A woman in her late 60s invited them in and introduced herself. She was Gladwyn Bush, she said, but everyone called her Miss Lassie. When Miss Lassie excused herself to go to the kitchen, which was a little separate building in the lush yard behind the house, Sally's eyes had the opportunity to explore the interior of Miss Lassie's house. What she saw amazed her. Every surface was painted with scenes and figures: the walls, the woodwork, the floor, the doors, and the windows. The ceilings were painted dark and covered with stars. And everywhere there were cats, probably 20 of them, along with their fleas. Later Sally would have an opportunity to see Miss Lassie's kitchen house in which the refrigerator was covered with a life-sized painting of Jesus.

Over tea, Miss Lassie explained that she was born in Grand Cayman, a fourth generation Caymanian, and she had never been off the island. Her father had been a seafarer. She had lived in the house with her sister until her sister died. She alluded somewhat vaguely to a husband who was not well and lived on the island but not with her. Miss Lassie showed Sally the bed her father had made for her and the small organ she prized so highly. She was quite self-sufficient, harvesting food from her garden and fish from the ocean just across the way.

She had received all of her education from missionaries. It was a few years earlier, when she was just in her early sixties, that she'd had a religious vision that moved her deeply and impelled her to begin painting. She had no artistic training and painted with whatever she had, often house paint. The works she created were described as "primitive," with simple lines and bold colors and were almost exclusively depictions of Bible stories.

Sally was enchanted with Miss Lassie, her story and her artwork and asked if she might return. This was the beginning of a lovely association. And Sally, being the gifted and natural promoter of what is good began talking about this wonderful hidden treasure right there in Grand Cayman

Miss Lassie at her organ

Miss Lassie loved Ward and the fact that he would sing with her as she played the organ. And Sally loves to recall the image of Sunday mornings when a young man would push Miss Lassie's organ down the street with Miss Lassie trotting along beside it. Then after the service was finished, Sally would see them coming back.

Ward invited his barbershop quartet, "The Amazing Greys" and their wives, to come to the Caymans. One day they had stopped for a drink at the lounge of the Hilton Hotel that was nearly empty at the time. Something spontaneously happened amongst the guys that made them burst into song. They enjoyed themselves so much that one song led to another, and soon the whole space began filling to overflowing with appreciative listeners.

Word soon spread, and they received invitations to sing all over the island. They never charged for their performances, but if contributions were made to them, they always were redirected to help children in hospitals. The group accepted one invitation to sing at a Pentecostal church where people spoke in tongues. The wife of one of the devout Catholic members of the quartet leaned over to Sally to say that her husband thought it was all so bizarre that he was worried he might now be destined for Hell.

Each year when Sally returned to the Caymans she brought canvases, paints, and fruitcake for her friend, Miss Lassie. Miss Lassie just loved fruitcake! And as more and more people came to see Miss Lassie's work for themselves, they too spread the word until Miss Lassie became a well-known and celebrated figure in the art world of the

Caymans. She was eventually honored with recognition of MBE, member of the Order of the British Empire in 1997. Unfortunately Miss Lassie developed cataracts but was too fearful of leaving the island to go for medical treatment and eventually lost her vision. She died in 2003 but left for posterity a museum on Grand Cayman dedicated to her works. Miss Lassie gifted Sally with one of her paintings. The museum was happy to purchase it from her for $2,000 for their collection.

Miss Lassie's gift to Sally

53 - Dom Perignon

Friends Shirley and Chuck from Sally and Ward's duplicate bridge group in Lincoln. Nebraska also joined them in the Caymans. Betty, Shirley and Sally were at lunch at a restaurant on Grand Cayman when a fellow at the bar asked to buy them a drink and join them. They simply acknowledged that they had heard the offer but declined. Still he persisted, suggesting he would order them a bottle of Dom Perignon. One of the women said with dismissive sarcasm that they'd take him up on that offer, and sure enough, the waitress brought the Dom Perignon and glasses to their table, followed by the man who pulled up a chair. He bantered on and then invited them out on his boat. They laughed that they would have to check with their husbands. He said he was not interested in their husbands. Then to Sally's great embarrassment, he zeroed in on Sally. He said she looked like his wife. When Shirley picked up her camera to take a picture to laugh about later, a thuggish looking guy who seemed to be closely watching what was going on shook his head no. But the man dismissed the thug's disapproval and posed for the picture, telling the women his name. Shortly after that, the women left, saying they were meeting their husbands.

Sally in the Caymans

The photo was forgotten until many months later. Sally was watching " America's Most Wanted," a program she rarely watched, and there on the screen was the face of the guy in the Caymans with the Dom Perignon. And under the photograph was the man's name, the same name he had used when he introduced himself to them. It turns out he was a notorious drug boss, and the FBI was searching for him. They requested any clues or information from the public about his whereabouts. Sally picked up the phone and called Shirley to see if she still had the picture she had taken with her camera, and she did. They sent the FBI the picture of the man, the details of the encounter, and when and where it took place. "Just imagine," they rolled their eyes, "what could have happened if we'd taken him up on the boat ride as well as the Dom Perignon!" They never heard any more of what became of the man, and that was fine with them.

54 - A Springboard From Spirit Lake

Sally had managed to keep Tonsfeldts in Spirit Lake functioning, but business there and in the country as a whole wasn't thriving. Wayne Crim had grasped an opportunity to buy at a cheap price a line of crude furniture made of large roots and other rescued wood that was refinished and equipped in some cases with cushions. The introduction of these pieces embarrassed the designers; the contrast with Tonsfeldt's classic, dignified reputation could not have been more stark. He placed the pieces in the show windows, but none of it sold, and business lagged further.

The decorators lamented how few customers they had coming into the store, and Sally even dressed as a clown to make it fun to visit Tonsfeldt's. But business continued to be sluggish. He suggested to the

Sally clowns for Tomsfeldt's

decorators that they get out and drive around Lake Okoboji with their windows down and listen for the sound of hammers echoing around the lake. Where there was construction, there could be customers. , but business continued So Sally took her own advice and went to Lake Okoboji where she did hear hammers. While trying to track them down she quite incidentally ran into a woman by the name of Joan Kirke, and the two had a pleasant conversation about nothing in particular. Then a few days later Joan Kirke came into Tonsfeldts and recognized Sally. She told Sally that she'd let her young kids paint the bathroom of the cottage they'd rented. They'd spilled paint on the carpet that she now needed to replace. Sally helped her with the new carpet, which was not a large or expensive purchase. Sally assumed Joan was just a nice, average, person, not a person of wealth. But though Sally didn't know it, she had established a contact that would prove remarkably beneficial.

Joan then called Sally and asked Sally to meet her at Lake Okoboji. When Sally arrived, the house where they met was not at all the modest one she expected. It was brand new, extremely large and lavish, with a guesthouse that had three bedrooms. She asked Sally if she would be interested in undertaking the designing and decorating of the properties. Sally was delighted and said of course she would. The furnishing would be purchased from Tonsfeldts, and the store was quite blown away with Sally's major coup.

Joan Kirke's husband Gary was the partner of Bill Van Orsdel. The two had been high school friends in Des Moines who met again a decade later in 1974 and decided to go into business together. They started the insurance brokerage firm Kirke-Van Orsdel Inc., and the business took off like a rocket. Within their first ten years the firm had joined forces with a New York competitor and assembled a list of Fortune 500 clients.

It was in that ten-year window of burgeoning success that Sally met Joan Kirke. Sally was never entirely sure about the exact nature of their business, but she knew it involved a great deal of money. Kirke-Van Orsdel Inc. had a vault protected around the clock by armed security guards, and the company even had its own zip code. Sally was pleased that Gary Kirke was happy to spend some of that money with her. Word got to Gary Kirke that Sally had referred to him as "Mr. Mega Bucks," and he found it totally amusing - not the least offensive. He even

A Complete Retreat

Article by Mary Hutchison Tone
Photos by Joan Liffring-Zug

When Gary Kirke, chairman of the board and chief executive officer of Kirke-VanOrsdel, Incorporated (see pp. 26-27) wants to relax, he heads to Lake Okoboji. Here, Kirke, head of the eighth fastest-growing, privately-held company in the country, frequently unwinds, combining business with pleasure. It is not unusual for him to spend a weekend working in one of his three northwestern Iowa insurance offices while enjoying summertime activities with his family at their spacious summer home on West Lake Okoboji.

Built in 1965 by Earl Hoover and his wife, Bonnie, (she was a Pillsbury), this three-story, six-bedroom home situated on Fairoaks Beach mixes elegance with informality. It's a match that well suits Kirke, his wife, Joan, and their four children, Gary Jr., 12, Charlie, 7½, Tim, 5, and Jonna, 4.

Kirke acquired the home in 1980 from Rich Reimers when Kirke-VanOrsdel purchased the Peters-Reimers Insurance firm with offices in Spencer, Milford, and Spirit Lake.

"This home is the perfect place for us," says Kirke. "My family loves it

here in the summer. It's convenient for me since I need to spend some time up at the lake offices; and we felt that, by living here, we'd be making a commitment to the community — something we like to do since we own a business here." (Kirke's partner, Bill VanOrsdel, and his wife, Elaine, also have a home on West Lake Okoboji.)

Joan Kirke supervised the choice of decor throughout the house. She was assisted by a Denver (Colorado) designer, Sally Beightol, who was then employed by a Spirit Lake furniture store, Tonsfeldts. "We wanted to

Seated in the living room of their summer home at Lake Okoboji are Gary and Joan Kirke, and their four children: (from left) Tim, 5; Jonna, 4; Charlie, 7½; and Gary, Jr., 12. Photo by Marvin Burk Photography, Spencer.

sometimes enjoyed referring to himself that way.

Despite his massive success, he was very down to earth, and he worked hard. The Kirkes were so pleased with the work Sally had done on the Lake Okoboji house and guesthouse that they asked her to undertake redoing their Victorian mansion on a hill in Des Moines. This new opportunity presented itself just at the end of the two-year commitment at Spirit Lake that Sally had with Wayne Crim. She was now at liberty to freelance. Joan told her that her husband's sister-in-law was supposedly working on plans for the house but that she was clearly not picking up on Gary's preferences for furnishing and style. They could see that there would be no such problem with Sally. Sally accepted, and a beautiful spread highlighting her work on the Des Moines house appeared in The Iowan magazine..

This led Gary Kirke to engage her to decorate three apartments he rented on the top floor of a fancy hotel in Des Moines and maintained for special customers and out-of-town guests. He saw to it that Sally and Ward were given a beautiful apartment for the month or so that it took Sally to transform the apartments. It was great fun.

1982...
Ups and Downs
Downs and Ups

55 - Designer Network

When Sally returned to Denver, she was ready to initiate a new business. She would call it Designer Network and locate it where Coors Stadium now stands. At the same time, the prestigious International Society of Interior Designers was just getting started, and Sally decided to apply. She interviewed with different people and was tested and

ISID

International Society of Interior Designers

This is to Certify that

Sally Ann Beightol

was admitted to

Professional Membership
Charter Member, Rocky Mountain Chapter

Date   President
April 1988

required to create a project. But because she was a professional already working in the field, she was allowed to forego certain classes and other requirements and was initiated in as one of its earliest members. Having the initials "ISID" after her name was an important professional feather in her cap.

Designer Network would provide designers for a reasonable fee with office space, access to a single secretary who would facilitate their paperwork, a showroom of samples and catalogues for ordering wallpaper, paint and window coverings, as well as access to her "workroom" of skilled technicians. Sally would also teach classes for her designers and even feed them once a month, but the economy and the business climate continued to be sluggish. As a result, the Network drew few designers, and both Sally and the designers were still finding it necessary to do other work of their own on the side.

What she felt would be the pivotal piece in finally achieving success would be making it possible for Network designers to order furniture at wholesale prices from the major manufacturers. At the time, no designer could do this without first being an employee of a furniture store. Without that capability, independent designers were hamstrung in offering full service to their clients at competitive prices. If she could provide her designers this capability, she felt confident that Designer Network would surely take off.

Gary Kirke kept in touch with Sally. He had great confidence in her skills and was interested in her newest enterprise. The two discussed the missing piece that Sally saw in her new Network concept. Gary then talked with his best friend, Bill Artis, who owned a large and successful furniture store in Des Moines. Bill Artis agreed that the prospects for success of Sally's concept looked very promising all around, and he became the critical piece in bringing her full concept to fruition. The three of them each put up $25,000.00 and gained one-third ownership in Designers Network.

With Bill Artis onboard, Sally's designers had access to the catalogues of the major furniture manufacturers and could order items at wholesale prices through Bill Artis. The items would be delivered to Sally's warehouse, and Sally's company would retain 20% of the wholesale price of the orders. This was reasonable given the fact that retail furniture prices are normally marked up two and a half times their cost. Small independent designers would at last be able to compete on the playing field. This was reminiscent of Sally's dad's involvement with IGA, the Independent Grocers Association, which was an effort to level the playing field between the huge and small independent grocers.

But despite this added new capability, the economy was still in recession in the mid 1980s, and almost no one was building new homes or buying new furniture. Nor did the designers have the same fire in their bellies that Sally had to "go out and listen for hammers" or charmingly cultivate clients by discovering and filling their needs.

Instead, what was happening in the mid 1980s was that one builder and then another contacted Sally. These were builders who'd had very satisfying reciprocal relationships with Sally in the past. In the past they would hire Sally for a fee to design and then create models for them. The builder would pay for all the furnishings Sally needed for the models, and then Sally would make all arrangements for delivery and setting up. Then when the houses were no longer used as models, she would organize and publicize a sale on the site to sell the furnishings. Sally and the builder would each receive half of the proceeds, and Sally would take care of returning anything that remained.

Now these builders came to her pleading, "We're starving out here! Will you take my furniture and see if you can sell it?" She took some of it and moved it to a whitewashed basement with an elevator down to it. She took pieces out and put them in the offices of the designers in hopes of sales, but no one was buying.

So though Designer Network was a very good idea, the time for it wasn't right, and the business never got traction. It was the worst time and the worst economy for the concept to succeed." It turns out that even now so many years later independent designers still do not have access to order furniture through major manufacturers without first having a direct connection with a furniture store.

56 - Second Time Around Becomes Model Home Furniture

Then one desperate builder gave her complete access to his whole warehouse of furniture, hoping she could magically sell pieces, but it didn't happen. Nothing moved, and all Sally could think to do was to open the warehouse to the pubic and call it "Second Time Around."

Warehouse of furniture from model homes

So Designer Network failed completely, but the time and the economy were perfect for "Second Time Around." It was incorporated in December of 1986, and it took off, leading to the incorporating of a second store, the Broadway store, in 1988. When Sally got repeated calls to the "Second Time Around" numbers inquiring about used wedding gowns, she knew she needed a more apt name for her business.

When she opened her third store she named it "Model Home Furniture" and then converted the name of the first two as well. Model Home Furniture was a more descriptive name for a warehouse that sold appealing furniture that had been displayed in the model homes of builders.

Sally and a new Model Home Furniture Store

With this new successful venture, Sally asked Gary Kirke and Bill Artis if they would like their interests in Designer Network transferred instead to Model Home Furniture, but they thanked her and declined.

As Model Home Furnishing was taking off, Ralph was just finishing college. Sally encouraged him to come and join her in its growth, and he did. The business was a great collaboration between Ralph and Sally. The business had three salaried personnel: Ralph, the bookkeeper and a worker in the warehouse. Sally and the other sales personnel worked on straight commission. This allowed Sally the flexibility to continue to work in another of her businesses, Sally B Designs. She did design work for private clients as well as designing models for builders.

Ralph and Sally had a wonderfully productive ten years together. Sally loved Ralph's presence and how thoroughly he learned about the store's products so that rather than persuading customers as many salesmen did,

Advertisement for Model Home Furniture

he informed them, gave them the information on which to base their decisions.

Sally recalls with a smile how one day she was absolutely fit to be tied with some frustrating situation, and Ralph said to her, "Come with me, Mom." He led her to an office and sat her down and insisted it was now time that she learned to swear. "Just say, "____ it!!! Come on, Mom! Just say it. You'll feel so much better." "Oh, no. I can't," she shook her head, still seething. "Oh yes you can. Say "____ it!" he laughed. And she couldn't help laughing too, and she finally just followed his advice. And between the laughter and the swearing, she definitely felt better.

Their sales were so successful that Sally needed to actively go out and seek new sources for furniture to stock her stores.

Sally and Ralph, business partners

57 - 45th Class Reunion

1992 would be the year of Sally's 45th high school graduating class reunion. She had never returned to Ann Arbor for one of these events; life had come on so dramatically with college, romance, marriage, a baby and a second and then so many life-changing surprises including more babies and far-flung deployments and new occupations. This year, however, she was determined to go and take her mother who was 87 with her to visit again the places where they had both spent such memorable years.

Dick Snyder greeted Sally and her mother at the opening event of the class reunion. At first Sally didn't recognize Dick, but then the years simply fell away. He had been her childhood playmate and earliest sweetheart. And Dick had always had a special place in his heart for Minnie, and she for him. The three of them quickly established a warm, comfortable relationship in which they all felt perfectly at home. Dick and Sally had fun connecting with old friends as Minnie smiled on.

The agenda for the reunion was packed with activities. The group was listening to a poem written for the occasion by their classmate, Don Yates who had become a professor of English.

Sonnet to a Town

How do you write a sonnet to a town?
What line can capture twenty years of joy
That shaded streets and sledding-hills write down
On memory lists the years cannot destroy?

Do you evoke the image of a fall,
With sweet blue smoke and football days a part?
Or do you rouse that springtime to recall
When she you winter-skated broke your heart?

The gentle Huron River and the Arb.
The golf course where you trapped moles,
will this do?
A mention of great winters' timeless garb
On circling foothills. Could these be too few?

I beg you, knowing reader, to lend sympathy
To this attempt to praise Ann Arbor perfectly

Ed and his mom

It was greeted warmly with appreciative applause and nostalgic smiles. Then someone asked, "So Don, who was that girl who 'winter-skated broke your heart'?" He grinned, looking in Sally's direction, "It was Sally Meyer." She was speechless, astonished that someone would carry such a memory for over 40 years.

Sally's younger brother Ed dropped in on one event to see his mom and sister. He brought his beloved dog, Chester. Chester, he laughed, would leap into Ed's truck through the window whenever Ed was going anywhere. Dog lover that Dick was, he was crazy about Chester.

While they were in Ann Arbor, mother and daughter went to see their old home on Willow Street that Minnie had sold to two lawyers in 1979. The owners greeted them warmly and showed them through the house they had renovated into a marvelous and more modern home. They had redesigned the roof to accommodate great windows that illuminated the second floor. Minnie and Sally left filled with satisfaction that the home of their memories had been so lovingly adopted and honored.

When the events of the reunion concluded, the friends all went their separate ways after promising to meet again at the 50th

It was several months after Minnie accompanied Sally to her class reunion in 1992 that Sally found herself in Michigan again. This time it was to explore with her brother Ed his desire to establish a Model Home Furniture type business in Detroit and replicate the success Sally had had in Denver. Minnie had always encouraged Sally to help Ed when she could. Ed had even been pivotal in getting Sally underway in her first Hummel plaque business, so she was now happy to try to help Ed.

Ed was at a crossroads in his life and ready for a new direction. Substance abuse often afflicts dyslexics at a greater rate than those in the general populace, and the easy availability of alcohol in the restaurant industry magnifies its threat. Then that predisposition in Ed was multiplied by the diagnosis of his father's alcoholism. And as if this weren't enough, a hereditary psychiatric disorder in Sue's genetic line cropped up in two of their children. Their youngest child, John, was diagnosed with schizophrenia, and his condition required special supervision and treatment. In the face of all of this, Ed found himself severely challenged to maintain his equilibrium. At first alcohol seemed to help him cope, but then the alcohol gained the upper hand. It led to the end of Ed and Sue's marriage and the loss of many of good jobs. Now she saw that helping him extricate himself from his work in bars and restaurants could be key in his achieving a more promising future

When John was about ten, Ed had turned to his older sister proposing that she and Ward adopt their son, hoping that Ward with his background in psychology and his success in working with young men could provide the help John needed. But after much soul searching, they had to conclude that their complicated life with five children of their own and both parents working full time could not be the solution Ed needed for John. They simply could not take this responsibility and all it entailed with any hope of success.

Now in 1992, Ed was 55 and ready to begin a new direction in his life, Sally wanted very much to be able to help him this time get his life back on the rails. Their mother had asked Sally repeatedly to look out for her brother. Ed had purchased a building that he thought would work for a Model Home Furniture type business in Detroit, and he had invited Sally to help him initiate it. But she discovered to her great disappointment that conditions in the Detroit building industry were unlike those that had been so conducive to her success in Denver. In Detroit there were not major builders creating an ever-changing array of model homes that were generating an abundance of stylish furniture that could afterwards be sold to the public by an enterprising businessperson. In Detroit there were, instead, smaller operations run mostly by families. The large inventory of furniture from model homes was simply not there. It wasn't possible to replicate the concept without that inventory.

58 - Farewell Minnie

It was that same August of 1992 while Sally and Ed were focused on these matters in Michigan that they received a phone call saying that Minnie hadn't been feeling well for several days and now it was clear that she had suffered an aneurism. They were informed there was no surgery or protocol that promised a positive outcome. Sally and Ed sat beside her bed hoping against hope. Each time Minnie would cough they would think, "Oh, she' waking up," but she didn't. Minnie passed peacefully in her sleep within a week. What an enormous hole Minnie's death left in the hearts and lives of those who loved her. Ward was one of her admirers, always saying, "If you like the mother, you'll have a good marriage."

She and Frank, after both losing their spouses, enjoyed a very good ten years as a married couple. They were competitive card players and kept a running tab of their cribbage scores. Sally says her mother had always been "smart as a whip" about euchre, auction bridge, and cribbage. When Minnie died, she was 439 ahead of Frank. Frank had agreed to move to Denver from Spirit Lake so that Minnie could be closer to Sally and her family. Sally helped them find an apartment in a

Frank Flint and bride
Minnie Meyer Flint

senior living facility. It had a balcony, and Minnie could cook if she chose to or they could have meals provided. They made friends, and Frank was the caller for bingo. Minnie was delighted when she found that they would be able to have the facility's attractive model apartment. But when Sally went to see her mom there after she and Ward returned from vacation, Minnie was ready to move again. "Why, what's wrong?" Sally asked. Minnie replied, "They're dying out there," pointing out the window. It turned out that their window had a clear view of the exit through which each deceased resident was wheeled out and put into a waiting hearse. "But Mom," Sally said, "You know people are going to die some time." "I know," Minnie said, "but I don't want to watch it." So they moved again.

They made arrangements for Minnie's funeral to be held in Ann Arbor at Muhlig Funeral Home "where every German family in town had their funerals."Members of Sally and Ed's families attended along with many old friends from church and bridge, work and volleyball. Minnie's best friend Esther Schneider tucked a deck of cards in beside Minnie. guests. To this very day, one of Sally's great and regularly used treasures is her mother's cookbook in her very own handwriting.

Flint, Wilhelmina H. (Meyer)
Denver, CO
Formerly of Ann Arbor

Age 86, died Saturday, August 29, 1992 in Denver. She was born December 22, 1905 in Hancock, MI. Mrs. Flint had been a long time Ann Arbor resident. On July 28, 1928, she married Frederick C. Meyer, he preceded her in death July 3, 1977. She is survived by her husband, Frank P. Flint; daughter, Sally Beightol of Englewood, CO; sons, Ed Meyer of Michigan and John Flint of Connecticut; daughters, Betsy Holzhauer of Iowa and Tobie Smith of New York; 18 grandchildren; and 1 great-grandchildren. Funeral service will be held 11 a.m. Friday, September 4, 1992 at the MUEHLIG CHAPEL. Burial will follow at Forest Hill Cemetery. Memorial tributes may be made to Hope United Methodist Church 1501 S. Dayton St., Englewood, CO 80111. The family will receive friends at the chapel Thursday evening 8-

59 - Ed in Denver

Minnie's obituary

The busy year in which Sally celebrated her 45th class reunion, Ed began his search for a fresh start, and the family mourned the death of Minnie, concluded with Ward's milestone 70th birthday on December 17th. Everyone knew that Minnie would have been the first to celebrate Ward's birthday, so though a bit dampened, plans for the event went forward. After Minnie's death, Ed had decided to put his house on the market in Detroit and move to Denver.

He rented a house just down the street from Sally. One of her favorite memories of her brother is how perfectly he was in his element when he masterfully orchestrated the celebration of Ward's 70th birthday. The celebration involved the Mile High Chorus, and Ed demonstrated his wonderful capacity to make everything so much fun.

The year Ed moved to Denver, his second wife, Jackie, didn't accompany him, but he brought her son Sean whom Ed had adopted. He bought a delivery van with a plan to help the boy get started in Sally's business. But the boy was young, unskilled and without much of a work ethic. He didn't arrive on time, was reckless with the furniture and left the carpet of the customer dirty, violating the high standards Sally had taken such pride in maintaining in her business. With her reputation at stake, Sally couldn't afford to employ him and in doing so replace any one of the loyal, skilled movers who had worked for her for so long. Again she found herself struggling with hopes and expectations Ed held that seemed beyond her capacity to meet.

60 - By Sheer Coincidence

The next year, 1993, Ward and Sally were getting away for a vacation in Scottsdale, Arizona. Sally had done the decorating and furnishing of an office building for a woman named Barbara Parker. Barbara admired Sally's work, and made an arrangement with her to furnish and decorate her condo on a golf course in Scottsdale. In lieu of paying Sally, Sally would be entitled to vacation there, something she and Ward did for a number of years.

Ward spotted an ad promoting a casino that offered buckets of shrimp for $2.00. How great was that, lunch and a chance to do a little gambling? As they were walking through the casino, they heard someone calling Sally's name.

To everyone's startled amazement, there was Dick Snyder. He explained that he was in Arizona visiting his daughter who lived there. His daughter who was known then as Amy, but who later changed her name to Ehren, was there with him at the casino. Dick found her and introduced her to Ward and Sally.

Sally remembers discovering that she had actually known Amy/Ehren's mother Barbara in junior high school. The two had gotten into mischief together. Dick, Barbara and Amy/Ehren had moved to Arizona where they lived until Dick and Barbara divorced when their daughter was nine. Dick then moved back east.

Ward and Dick found they had many common interests and communicated enjoyably and well together. Dick asked Sally about Minnie and was saddened to learn that she had died. As they parted, Ward, Dick and Sally said they looked forward to being together again at the 50th class reunion four years later in 1997.

61 - Executor of Minnie's Will

Sally had been named executor of Minnie's will and, with the help of a CPA did her best to see that all was fairly and accurately managed. Two properties were involved. One was the small house across the street on Willow Street that Minnie had purchased when she moved to Denver. After she married Frank Flint, it remained a rental property until Pam and her kids moved in after she and John divorced in 1992 when their kids were in grade school.

Minnie's little house across the street

The other property was the rustic Michigan one in Montmorency County that they called the Meyer Camp. Ed pressed Sally to get a price for the Willow Street property, so Sally consulted a realtor in the area for a price. The agent gave her a price of $80,000 that she promptly conveyed to Ed. He subsequently selected the Michigan property, and Sally agreed to pay Ed the price difference.

After Ed received his share of Minnie's estate, his second wife, Jackie, divorced him, claiming a good portion of the inheritance as her rightful due. Ed was increasingly squeezed financially.

Then long after Minnie's estate had been settled, Sally was devastated to learn from her niece that her father, Ed, was telling the family that their Aunt Sally had cheated him out of $10,000.00. The issue revolved around the price of the Willow Street house in Denver. Ed was accusing Sally of deliberately low-balling the price to him, apparently so he would not choose it but instead the Michigan property.

Sally went back to the real estate agent who had given her the original numbers and asked about the discrepancy that her brother was raising. The agent stood by his numbers, saying those were indeed the numbers he'd given her but perhaps she could have gotten the numbers from an official assessment.

"I feel awful about this," she said to Ward. "I'm just going to give him the money." But Ward told her she needed to stand her ground. She had done nothing wrong or inappropriate, and to pay him $10,000.00 would be a violation of principle. What was truly the right thing to do, she still doesn't know. She could only understand it from her perspective since Ed never explained his. If there was a better resolution, they didn't find it. So the unresolved anger and feeling of hurt on both sides lingered for years.

62 - Pepper in the Soup

During the summer of 1993 Sally was involved in her Model
Home Furniture businesses and was asked as a professional designer to
write an informative piece for a Denver magazine. It addressed the
"secrets" of how to achieve "that 'put together' look you've seen in
designer models and special homes." She discussed the designer's
"secret formula" of 60% one color, 30% another color, and 9% accent.
And then there is the all-important "color surprise." It is the 1% added
to the balanced room that is unexpected and adds zest and delight, "the
pepper in the soup."

63 - Three Years in Virginia

In 1993 one of Sally's sales people at Model Home Furniture brought Sally a customer who wanted to be introduced to the owner. Her name was Kathy Astroth, and she explained she was working on a Master's degree in business and was intrigued by the nature of Sally's business. She said that that she was from Virginia and thought her community there would be a great location for a business such as Sally's. She wanted to explore with Sally whether she could come to Virginia to get such a business started.

This was something she and Ward needed to discuss because Ward had had several worrisome health episodes. While hunting with his brother Bob, he had stepped in a hole in just the wrong way and broken his leg. Then he was scheduled for minor foot surgery for a bunion, and the surgery went well but there was a reaction to the antibiotics he was given. To finally overcome the reaction, he was given a designer cocktail of antibiotics through a port under his clavicle that allowed him to at last turn the corner and get well. But essentially they all agreed that Ward was fine and that starting a new store in Virginia sounded like a perfect project for Sally.

Sally and Kathy Astroth then formed a partnership to create Model Home Furniture in Chantilly, Virginia, just 20 minutes from Dulles Airport in Washington, D.C. As soon as the agreement with Kathy was firm, Sally purchased a coupon offered by one of the airlines for $2000.00 that allowed her for a year to jump on a plane whenever she chose and go anywhere she wanted or needed to go. Ward would man the fort at home, but she would be able to fly home often to check on business and be with Ward and the family. And she would be able to pop up to visit Kristy and her family in Massachusetts.

It became apparent that Ward needed heart bypass surgery, and when all appeared stable during his convalescence, Sally returned to work in Virginia. Since Kathy Astroth was visiting in Denver during that time, she went by to see if she could be of any help to Ward. "As a matter of fact," Ward answered, "Yes, you can. The lawn really needs to be mowed. Could you do that?" "Of course," she replied, and they went to the garage and got out the mower. It started with a pull-rope, so she stepped up and energetically pulled it. The engine sprang to life, and since the control was in the "Forward - Full" position, the mower shot off across the yard as Kathy stood in stunned amazement. By the time she recovered her composure, it was heading at full throttle for the neighbor's yard. She ran after it, but it was outpacing her as it shot across that neighbor's yard and into the next as flabbergasted neighbors gaped. At last she caught up to it as neighbors shouted to her what to do to kill the engine.

"For Pete's sake, what happened?" Ward asked as she wheeled the lawnmower back. "Haven't you ever used a lawnmower before?" Kathy replied, "Well, no, but I thought it couldn't be all that hard." Ward took several deep breaths, relieved that it seemed the new bypass was still holding.

The day the store in Virginia was scheduled to open, Sally was waiting for someone with the keys to unlock the doors and noticed a woman looking in the windows. Sally told her the store would open in just a few minutes, and the two started to chat. The woman told Sally that she had a new house that she was eager to fix up. Sally asked quite offhandedly, "You don't happen to have an apartment in your new house that you're thinking about renting, do you?"

"Well," she answered. "As a matter of fact I do,"

The two made arrangements for Sally to come and take a look. She found a townhouse full of moving boxes but also with a very fine lower level with a large room, a bedroom and a bathroom. As things turned out, it worked beautifully with Sally sharing the kitchen. And this is how she came to know Pat Scott who became a wonderful wonderful friend.

Ward bought Sally a used but very serviceable car and drove it to Virginia to give her more flexibility there. Ward took great pride in never buying new cars. His frugal upbringing stayed with him his entire life, so when a new car was needed, they went to the lot where Hertz sold its used rental cars. Keys would be on the tops of each in the lot, and they would pick up and try one and then another until they found one they thought would work for them.

Sally lived In Pat's townhouse apartment in Reston the three years she was in Virginia. When Ward or the kids or friends came, there was enough room for them to stay. From the townhouse it was an easy drive to public transit where they would park the car and zip to Washington, D.C. to explore its many attractions.

One of the perks Ward was eligible for as a retired military officer was to be able to fly standby at no cost anywhere in the world. Sally was eager to be able to just flip a coin and pick up and go. Once they were empty nesters, she bought an international time-share so they would have accommodations where they traveled, but Ward was not as enthusiastic as she was.

64 - Steamboat Springs

On one of her visits home, she and Ward found and fell in love with a beautiful condo in the ski community of Steamboat Springs, Colorado. Ward had at last recovered from several issues with his health, and the two were looking forward to again being able to be together with family and friends and participate in the great camaraderie they always so much enjoyed. The property up Troublesome Creek Road had long been a gathering place for this kind of fun, but now it had grown impractical. It was a challenge to get there, and there were few amenities when they did. When they saw the condo at Steamboat Springs they realized how very nice it would be to have more comfort and easier accessibility as well as wonderful skiing. They decided to sell their beloved remote property and the Winnebago and invest. Everyone was delighted.

Being the natural business woman she was, Sally also realized that it made financial sense to allow trusted friends and friends of friends to rent it during the times the family wouldn't be using it. In very much the same way, Ward and Sally and their friends had rented Betty and Harry Munson's place in the Caymans for many years. So Sally and Ward created an attractive brochure showing off the charm and delight of the area and the condo and sent copies off with personalized notes to their friends. With Sally's 50th high school graduation coming up in 1997, she sent them to ten friends from school, one of which went to Dick Snyder.

65 - Business Shenanigans

While Kathy continued work on her Master's degree she appointed her neighbor Joy to be the first manager of the store. After a year, Joy wanted to get back to her design work and suggested that her daughter Nina be hired to take over as manager. Nina, her husband and children were currently living with Joy, and Nina was pregnant. The store did its best to accommodate Joy's and her daughter's wishes. Nina was paid her full salary for three months until she was ready to take over full time. Then when she brought the baby to work with her, everyone did their best to work around that. In addition the store paid for her to attend classes to make her aware of business scams that could be perpetrated if businesses were not watchful.

Things seemed to run smoothly for some time after she became manager until the inventory revealed concerning discrepancies. What became apparent was that numerous small checks for accessory items would not be submitted to the bookkeeper for months. Then at the time a large item was sold that equaled the total of the small checks, only then would the small checks be submitted, giving the appearance on the books that payment had been made for the large item. And the books appeared to balance. But when the inventory was conducted, pages and pages of accessory items were missing totaling $35,000.00. This was a sizable loss for a business just getting underway.

The only person with responsibility for and access to these elements was the store manager. Sally found it bitterly ironic that in having arranged for the new manager to have training in detecting and deterring fraud, the new manager then used what she had learned to defraud the very business that was entrusted to her care. Sally called the police, saw that a capable lawyer was hired, and sought justice in the courts.

This was the time that she was hearing more and more often from her kids at home that Ward was ill and not improving. He had gotten a cold that had turned into pneumonia. He was in the hospital but could be given no antibiotics because the previous ones he had been given had burned out his immune system. They urged Sally to come home.

Then the lawyer who was so committed to and well versed in the store's fraud case informed them that she was pregnant but also assured them that this would not interfere in her management of the case. In retrospect, Sally thinks she should have postponed the trial, but the lawyer was so good, the case was so clear, the significant people were there and prepared to testify - they were ready! AND she was needed ASAP in Denver. Then the day the case went to trial, the lawyer unexpectedly went into labor. Her firm appointed to replace her another lawyer who knew nothing about the case.

What was even more unbelievable was what Sally discovered later - that the judge in the case was in fact Joy's next-door neighbor, the mother of the defendant. Sally was called to testify first and asked one question: "Was this theft discovered in the course of the store's daily routine?" Sally answered, "No. It was discovered by examining the inventory records." Immediately, and without adding further explanation as to the reasoning behind his decision, the judge pounded his gavel and announced, "Case dismissed!" Sally, Kathy Astroth, and the bookkeeper sat in stunned disbelief as Nina smiled.

After the dismissal of the case, Kathy Astroth's corporate lawyer advised her that she should now have nothing more to do with this business she had appealed to Sally to come to Virginia and establish. Her lawyer told her it was the safest way to guarantee she would suffer no financial losses. She apologized to Sally, saying how much she admired her and wanted to be like her when she grew up, but she was giving the business back to Sally to make the decisions about what to do next. She would have nothing more to do with it.

Sally determined she needed to sell the business. It seemed most expedient if the staff who had worked the store could purchase it. She assured them that she was willing to work with them to reach an extremely reasonable and affordable arrangement that would allow them to comfortably assume its ownership.

Since Sally had started Second Time Around years before, she had always had a policy that allowed her employees to buy anything from her stores at half price. It was a perk that was used and valued but certainly had never been abused. But one unscrupulously ambitious saleswoman who had worked in the Virginia store saw her brazen opportunity. Why bother to buy Sally out when you can have Sally's cake and eat it too? She rented a space up the street, legally bought and paid for any and all of the interesting items in Sally's store. Then she borrowed a truck and transported it all to her store up the street, leaving Sally little to sell, the rent to pay for another year, and her husband critically ill in Denver. Now Sally realizes she should have proactively had a non-compete clause when she hired her staff, but, alas, she'd innocently trusted people to do the right thing. So up the street the woman was employing Sally's concept and techniques and selling Sally's merchandise while even making use of Sally's staff - and gloating because she'd been so clever. Of the challenges in Sally's life, this was the one in which she felt most devastatingly alone.

Again Sally prayed. A fellow she had known through the business who found her business concept interesting made an offer to buy the store, and she accepted it. Though little actual money changed hands, he took over the rent and responsibilities, and Sally was able to close the last brutal chapter of what had been a wonderful time in Chantilly, Virginia.

66 - A Smile and Then He Was Gone

Now it was November of 1996, and Sally was back in Denver. The hospital was reporting that at last things had begun to look up for Ward. The pneumonia had been very serious, but it was clearly looking as though Ward was going to be able to beat it despite the fact that there was no antibiotic that they could give him.

Ward had months before gotten tickets for Sally and him to go on a Barefoot Sailing Cruise for a week with the barber shoppers. Sally had concluded that the tickets simply would go unused with Ward in the hospital, but Ward now disagreed. He insisted that Sally should take Pam and go. They would have a great time, and Sally would benefit from some rest and fun. He assured and then reassured them that it would be fine. He was clearly on the mend and was ready to move on to rehab in a day or so. By the time Pam and Sally returned, he'd be coming home. "Go!" he smiled. "He was a happy boy," Sally said. So they kissed him good-bye and went home to pack their bags for their departure in the morning. But then there was the call with the dreaded words, "heart failure ... gone."

Karen and Sally spoke of the insistent demands for the family to make logical decisions in the midst of their shock and grief. But they also treasured the tiny, inexplicable surprises that felt like reassuring gifts from the playful Ward. They were in the car trying to decide when to hold the funeral when a date in the future inexplicably popped up on the car's screen. They thanked Ward and set it as the date.

Then "Wardie," Sally's pet name for Ward, suddenly appeared on the license plate of a car that slipped in in front of them in traffic. It felt for all the world as if Ward was happily waving, "Hi!" from the cockpit of his plane.

The family planned a wonderful, moving commemoration of Ward and his remarkable life. At Hope Methodist Church, the 100-voice, Mile High Chorus of which Ward was a long-time member, sang with soaring power and beauty. David's son Carson played his horn and his son Cole spoke of his grandfather. David played the guitar as Kris sang. Someone near Sally leaned over to say, "My God! I didn't know you were the Beightol von Trapp family!"

The minister focused her message on the word "virga" that

Pam's son Eric had brought to her attention. He told her that before and after school each day he went across the street to his grandparents' house because his mom's working hours at Craig Hospital started early and ran late. Each afternoon as he came in the door, his grandfather would have waiting for him a provocative question or an unusual word to stimulate his thinking and give them something to chew on together. The last word he selected for Eric was the word "virga." Eric discovered that "virga" is the word for the streaks of rain that appear under a cloud but evaporate before they reach the ground. The concept provided such a fertile analogy for comprehending aspects of life, and it was a most apt parting gift for a young grandson from his grandfather. The loss of his grandfather was particularly difficult for Eric.

Ward had been fascinated with the idea of flying for as long as he could remember. It had inspired him and his pal Bud Hovland to build a plane from scraps and pilfer an awning to create a skin for it. So a supreme moment of Ward's life was when decorated Colonel Willis Beightol, flew in to Ward's flight school graduation and with pride and great solemnity pinned the wings onto his brother's chest.

The ceremony included the magnificent poem **High Flight** by John Magee:

"Oh, I have slipped the surly bond of earth,
And danced the skies on laughter-silvered wings;
Sunward I've climbed and joined the tumbling
     mirth of sun-split clouds –
And done a hundred things You have not dreamed of –Wheeled and soared and
swung high in the   sunlit   silence.
Hovering there I've chased the shouting wind along
And flung my eager craft through footless halls of air
Up, up the long delirious burning blue
I've topped the wind-swept heights with easy grace
Where never lark, or even eagle, flew;
And, while with silent, lifting mind I've trod
     the high untrespassed sanctity of space,
     put out my hand and touched the face of God."

Ward was in his element behind the controls of a plane just as he was cultivating his garden or singing behind a microphone or competing in a bridge tournament or mentoring his brilliant young grandson. And he was always modestly understated about his achievements. Many of his fellow barbershoppers who had known him for years told Sally how astonished they were to learn the amazing details and accomplishments of his life.

The Beightols' good friend Judy Beckvermeth took charge of feeding everyone after the service. She had distributed little slips of paper to those she knew were coming to the funeral, each with a request to please bring a plate of this or that Mexican dish. The food was plentiful, Mexican, and delicious.

A fitting and joyful tribute to a good man.

199

1996...
A Dear Old Friend and
a New Beginning

67 - Picking Up the Pieces

Their house felt remarkably empty without Ward, and Sally hated rattling around there by herself while Pam and the kids were renting the house across the street.

She and Ward had already initiated work to put in hardwood floors, renovate the kitchen and make other improvements because they would then be able to write off the improvements if they were done because it was to be used as a rental property. Then Pam and the kids would be their renters. In 1996 after Ward died, Pam, Sarah, Erik, and Summer the golden retriever moved across the street to join Sally and create a new three generation family unit.

68 - Dick Snyder Writes Back

Dick Snyder

Not long after the funeral, Sally was going through the mail and discovered a response from Dick Snyder to the brochure she'd sent about the place at Steamboat Springs. He admired Steamboat but lamented that he didn't ski. He sent his regards to Ward and also included a paragraph for him about something they'd discussed and saying how much he'd enjoyed meeting him in Arizona and was looking forward to all being together again in Ann Arbor. Through her tears, Sally wrote back to Dick saying that Ward had died unexpectedly. Then after only as long as it would take for mail to get to Michigan, her phone rang, and it was Dick. He spoke with such compassionate concern for Sally and her loss. He stepped in as the bulwark he had always proved himself to be from the time they were childhood friends in Ann Arbor. Hoping to give her something positive to look forward to, he spoke of the reunion. He talked about the friends they had known together who had built houses near where he had also built at a lake in northern Michigan. Perhaps she might come and see his place, meet his dog Sam and Tiger the cat, and they could get together with their friends there. He planted seeds that helped Sally begin to see beyond the deep sadness that filled her.

69 - Lots of Work in a Healthy Economy

Sally B

Sally dealt with her grief by throwing herself into her work. She went out and found designing jobs, recognizing gratefully how much the economy had improved. Before the downturn she had done model homes for four builders who were now pleased to work with her again. There were also competitions for the most successful models, and Sally relished participating in them. It was a tremendous amount of work, but it also focused her mind and energy. It was where she'd always shone, and she knew the routine. First she and the builder agreed upon a budget for Sally's designing, selecting all furnishings, ordering and following up. The builder needed to have totally completed the houses by a specified date in order for Sally to begin her work, and then all three houses needed to be completed simultaneously by Sally in time for the Home Builders Association Show. These shows were highly competitive events, and winning was a major feather in the builder's and the designer's caps. Sally would often be in arranging flowers and giving final touches right up until the doors of the show opened. Then after the models closed, Sally would see to the sale of the furnishings on site, with half of the profits going back to the builder, and the other half to Sally's. It worked like a charm.

Sally eventually also had 20 apartments in #1 Denver Place, a high-end enterprise with hotel rooms on the first 10 or so floors and apartments on the upper floors that Viacom and other companies rented for celebrities and executives. Sally was contracted to decorate and furnish the apartments. She would purchase the furnishings from Model Home Furniture and then receive rental payments for them for as long as they were desired. When the time was up or it was time to redecorate, Sally would be notified, and she would arrange for the furnishings to be sold, but often the owner would simply buy them. She provided such a unique and valuable service and developed such a fine reputation that for years it was as though, Sally laughs, " the money rolled in under the door."

She bought a 1989 Buick Reatta, the first new car that was personally her own in her entire life. It was stylish and fun to drive, and she thoroughly enjoyed it. She finally sold it in 2012 to the clay model artist who had designed it.

70 - At Last, The 50th Reunion in Ann Arbor

So neither Ward nor Minnie flew with Sally in 1997 to the Ann Arbor High School Graduating Class of 1947's Fiftieth Class Reunion. Sally's friend Gerry Hepner had invited Sally to stay with her for the weekend and picked her up at the airport.

Ed came to visit Sally and brought his new chocolate lab named Chester. Ed was glad to see Dick again whom he'd known as a kid, and Dick was absolutely crazy about Chester.

There was golf and a dinner party leading up to the reunion all the dancing and carrying on, and then there was a breakfast before everyone departed. It had fallen to Gerry Hepner to actually pay the final and very large bill for all of the event's festivities. Gerry extended her credit card anticipating no issue whatsoever, but it was declined, leaving her embarrassed and with no Plan B. But Sally pulled out her credit card, which was honored without question, so Sally paid for the reunion until Gerry paid her back the next day.

Sally and Dick

71 - Off to the North Woods

Dick's Forest Lake House

After the finale breakfast that marked the conclusion of the 50th reunion, Sally and Dick walked together to Dick's car for the 2½ hour trip to Dick's cabin in in northern Michigan. They were both just a bit nervous, not knowing exactly what to expect. When Sally had told her grown children that she was staying on after the reunion for several days to go with Dick to Forest Lake, Kristy was dumbfounded, "But Mother you can't just go off to the north woods with someone you haven't known for 50 years!" while Pam said, "Mom, go for it." Sally and Dick chattered about the weather, Ann Arbor and events from the reunion, and then a slightly awkward silence descended. It was Dick who broke the silence, saying to her, "I want to tell you something." She thought, "Oh, my. Now we'll begin the discussion about the elements of significance in our lives." Dick continued, "See that over there?" Sally looked where he indicated. "That device with the crisscrossed pipes is a back flow preventer. They're outside of neighborhood areas and painted different colors. They keep the sewage from backing up. You can keep an eye out for them." Sally smiled. After their paths had parted so many years before, Dick had gone on to a long and successful career as a civil

C'mon, Dick

engineer. His professional knowledge was always a fallback to be tapped if ever he felt a pause turning into an uncomfortable silence.

"I hope my house is clean," he said as they pulled up the drive of a charming, well designed, natural wood house with tall windows that looked out into the trees.It was located across the road from the lake. Dick explained with modest pride that he had designed the house himself. He had hired a woman to clean the house while he was gone.

Greeting him as he opened the door were his two bachelor housemates: his affable, loyal, affectionate and essentially undisciplined, yellow lab, Sam and his self-assured and single-minded cat, Tiger. Tiger had come into Dick's life many years before when he and his brother Jack were fly fishing near Kalamazoo, Dick felt something and looked down to see a tiny kitten trying to climb up his leg. He reached down and picked up the little guy, looking around to see where he might have come from and who the owner might be. There was no one for miles. "I guess you must be mine," he smiled.

Some years later Dick got Sam when he was a fluffy little blonde puppy. When Sam came into Tiger's life and territory, Tiger demonstrated the authoritative self-assurance of his feline ancestry and lorded it over Sam. It didn't matter that Sam grew exponentially bigger than Tiger. All Tiger needed to do was look directly at Sam, and Sam hid his head and whined. At first Sam moped and pouted when Sally came. He resented sharing Dick's attention with this stranger.

Dick's house had an upstairs loft bedroom where Sally would sleep and a small downstairs bedroom where Dick would sleep. He wanted to make it clear that he had made appropriate arrangements for this to be a "proper" visit.

Dick checked with his mail and messages and found that he had work that he needed to promptly expedite for the engineering firm in Ann Arbor that he continued to do consultant work for. He apologetically asked Sally if she would be able to entertain herself while he took care of the work, and she replied, "Of course!" He got to work and she went upstairs to unpack. Closets ran the length of one nine-foot wall. When Sally opened them to hang up her things, she saw that two long shelves ran the full length of the closet, and each held stacks of three sweaters each, side by side from one end of the closet to the other. They were in a variety of sizes that matched Dick's physical size at the time he acquired each, a history of his life in sweaters. Before parting with many of them later to make room for her things, Sally got to hear the stories that went with many of the sweaters. A beautiful University of Michigan one had been gifted to him by an admirer but was too small for him anymore; however, it fit Sally perfectly, and Dick happily made it hers.

In their junior high yearbook, Dick was voted not only "best dressed boy," but also "most popular boy." He had a finely tuned appreciation of color and style. During the years he attended Michigan, he'd worked at Fiegles Men's Store in downtown Ann Arbor where he developed an eye for quality and refined his taste and style. Sally is sure that if Dick had not been expected and encouraged to pursue a career in civil engineering, his true choice would have been to be the owner and operator of a fine haberdashery. Professionally he was a very good civil engineer and found the work gratifying, but it didn't inspire in him the easy, "at-homeness" he felt when he stepped into a good men's clothing store. But following that desire, he decided, just "wouldn't be right." The men in his family were engineers.

After getting unpacked, Sally headed downstairs to see what she could find in the kitchen to fix them for lunch. His bachelor kitchen was so small that there was no room for two people to eat there. Around the corner and across the hall there was a table in the great room that could be used. She admired the house, but couldn't help noting how it might be improved.

While she was cleaning up after lunch, she discovered a hamper stuffed with dirty clothes, towels and bed linen that the cleaning woman had left there. Sally made herself useful by taking care of the laundry. Later on they got together with high school friends who had also built at Forest Lake, and they had a great time.

72 - Dick's Life After He and Sally "lost each other" After Junior High

Dick in the Navy

Dick had gone into the Navy after graduating from the University of Michigan in Civil Engineering, a career path designed to link well with Snyder Excavating, the business that had been in his family since before there were cars - from a time when their equipment was pulled by horses. The company dug many of the foundations for the structure of the University of Michigan and it had supported the entire extended family through the Depressiln the Navy Dick was stationed in Japan where he worked getting factories back up and running so that the economy could become functional again after the war. During the time he was there he had a meaningful 2-year romantic relationship with a Japanese woman, but he did not ask her to marry him because his mother made it clear that she would never be accepted because of the family's lingering animosity for the Japanese after WW II.

Financially the Snyder family business was not in very good condition when Dick returned. He went to work and successfully cultivated new business that stood to put the business back on its feet. But many bills and taxes were seriously delinquent, and without enough money coming in yet to stay ahead of them, the equipment and the business were lost. It broke Dick's heart.

Dick had started seeing a girl, Barbara Mercina, he had known from his school days. She was appealingly quirky and unpredictable, an interesting counterbalance for his naturally more controlled sensibility. She had been married and had a daughter who was about two. She and Dick decided to get married. Dick was hired to engineer a project to build a road to Grand Mesa in Colorado. There, Barbara established a successful practice in psychiatric counseling. They purchased a modest but very nice home there, and during that time their daughter Amy was born. Dick was 31. The year was 1960. Strains continued to grow in the marriage, and when Amy was nine, her parents divorced.

After several years as a bachelor, Dick still envisioned a life as a married man with a family. He met another woman, an organist at the church he attended, and somewhat impulsively the two decided to marry. But then after about a year it was necessary for Dick to take a new job out of state, and she did not want to leave her life and start anew someplace else. They agreed it made most sense to agree to simply go their separate ways again.

Then he met and married a very good woman named Helen who had a grown daughter named Brenda. Brenda and Dick happily "adopted each other," and Brenda and Ehren enjoyed each other as well. Dick's mother liked Helen very much, pleased that her son had chosen well. The marriage was happy and successful for several years, but then sadly Helen died of cancer.

Dick understandably began to feel as though perhaps marriage just wasn't for him. As he was nearing retirement, he designed and built for himself a bachelor pad at Forest Lake. He also decided to pursue an interest he had long held in painting and signed up for an art class, which he thoroughly enjoyed. He was especially drawn to watercolor, a wonderful medium that allowed him to express his love of color and

Dick's art

212

design as he found it in the landscape. With the eye of the artist and the attention to detail of the engineer, he created beauty.   He remained astonishingly humble about his work. He loved enrolling in art classes, learning new techniques and being with others as they created.

He had a number of female friends – ones with whom he golfed; others with whom he played bridge or went dancing. He regularly corresponded with some, but he had remained a bachelor for eleven years. Sally asked him why he hadn't remarried again, and he said, "I guess I was just waiting for the right woman. I was waiting for you." Sally had to conclude that that could be a line, but it was the best line she'd ever heard.

73 - A Couple Again?

As the week Sally spent with Dick at Forest Lake after the reunion was coming to a close, the friends and Dick insisted that Sally really must come back for the Ox Roast! They explained that it was a great community get together of all property owners at the lake. A committee would see to the slow roasting of the beef, which apparently because it sounded more exotic was called "ox," beginning very late at night and often accompanied by numerous Bloody Marys. Then everyone arrived at midday to set up their tables for the feast and to enjoy cakewalks, games, drawings, camaraderie and fun. Sally decided she would enjoy coming back. As Dick drove her downstate to catch her flight, they made plans for her next trip.

Sally definitely needed to get back to Denver because she had work waiting for her. She needed to complete three models she had gotten underway before leaving for the reunion. She had been trying to cope with pain in her hip that increasingly impeded her busy productive days. She went to the doctor who told her she needed a hip replacement, so she put her name on the waiting list. Having finished the models, Sally returned to Forest Lake for the Ox Roast. Dick's friends, the Booths, whom Sally hadn't yet met were coming to the lake to visit. Dick Booth said he knew right away that "Sally must be okay because she had frozen peas on her hip and a martini in her hand."

The strong, trustworthy, mutually respectful, and admiring relationship Sally and Dick had known as youngsters resumed in fuller form, refined by their separate experiences over the intervening 50 years. Their easy companionship was founded in the deep sense they both felt of "being home" again when they were in each other's company. They had so much in common – they read the same books, enjoyed doing the same things, went to the same church, and had the same political leanings.

With Sally still working in Denver, there were many flights back and forth. First Dick paid for one, then Sally the next, Dick the next and so on until they decided it was getting ridiculously expensive. Didn't it make perfect sense for them to get married? Sally could draw to a close her active work in Denver while long-term rental arrangements she had set up could easily continue remotely.

There was one practical consideration. As Ward's widow, Sally was entitled to continue his excellent health insurance benefits as well as the access she had enjoyed for so many decades to the governmental commissary and Base Exchange of the military. These had allowed her to save a great deal of money. If she married Dick, these benefits would be lost.

They discussed matters at great length, but Dick simply couldn't move beyond his sense that it "just wouldn't be right" ethically to put aside their obligation as role models for her grandchildren because the alternative was financially more expedient. Sally noted with a sigh that she only seemed to fall in love with bright, highly ethical men. "I would probably have gone to hell if it weren't for two proper guys," she added with a chuckle,

They saw that if they married, there would be some costs, but they also found silver linings. They found a reputable doctor who practiced on both sides of the American/ Canadian border. By making field trips to nearby Windsor on the Canadian side of the Detroit River every month or so, they could fill prescriptions for the same drugs at a fraction of what they would have to pay in the United States.

While they were there, they could have a little fun at the casinos and go to a favorite food truck that served delicious fish and chips with malt vinegar, a Canadian combination they very much enjoyed.

Yes, it would work.

And so in the invitation to their wedding, they included the words of Robert Browning:

> Grow old along with me
> The best is yet to be,
> The last of life, for which the first was
> made;
> Our times are in His hands
> Who saith, "A whole I planned,
> Youth shows but half…"
> Trust God:
> See all
> Nor be afraid!

74 - The Wedding Celebrations

They married in the backyard of the Willow Street home in Denver, where Pam had planted Sally's favorite red geranium and purple petunias. The day was hot, the smiles of the assembled family and friends broad, and the bride and groom radiant.

The family borrowed the cross from the church and positioned it atop the tall, narrow sofa table from the house. Summer, the golden retriever, was Sally's "darling" bridesmaid. Dick's daughter Ehren (formerly known as Amy) had brushed and groomed Summer until her coat shone. Summer located herself right under the table-altar near Sally, looking on with perfect composure, her paws crossed. Pam created a magnificent tiered wedding cake that she trimmed with fresh pansies.

The music was unbelievably wonderful. The Classic Collection, a remarkably gifted group of four young barber-shoppers, lovingly filled the celebration with song. Ward had been their coach and mentor, and they had gone on to win the International Grand Championship, the most highly esteemed of all Barbershop competitions. It was a remarkable afternoon.

Pam decorating the wedding cakes with pansies

The Classic Collection

217

The bride and groom
July 18, 1998.

The delighted Beightols with Mr. and Mrs. Snyder

Not long after, at Forest Lake there was a second reception with their Forest Lake friends, Dick's colleagues on the Board and others from Michigan. Most of the family was able to make the trip, and Pam created an encore of her wonderful pansy-decked cake for this celebration too.

Then a year afterward, Pam married David Lee, and they purchased the Willow Street house from Sally.

75 - Florida

Dick not only had his place at Forest Lake he also had one in Florida. One long winter several years earlier he was eager to find a respite from the cold northern winters. He headed for Florida where he found a very nice place, played a round of golf, and put down a deposit. As he continued down the road, he found one he liked even more and put a deposit on it too. Then his friend Dick Wagner who lived in Clearwater advised Dick to go to see Forrie Knapp at a golf community called Shalimar. Forrie was the sales agent there and was also a neighbor of Dick Snyder's at Forest Lake. So Dick Snyder went to meet Forey Knapp who found him a place at Shalimar that he liked even more than the other two. It was his final choice.

When Dick took Sally there, she quickly embraced the easy winter climate, the golf course and the pleasant layout of Dick's house. but she was greatly disappointed with its dated, avocado Herculon interior. That first winter she and Dick were living there, a friend from Clearwater named Dick Wagner dropped by for a visit. He was on the lookout for a house for himself and his partner. He arranged to see properties, and Sally went along while Dick Snyder drove to Lakeland to buy tickets for them all for a Detroit Tigers training camp ballgame. They were shown a model of a new design that was located on the golf course overlooking the water. It was definitely appealing but

considerably more expensive than the fine serviceable one which Dick had bought.

That night Sally couldn't sleep. She kept thinking about the model she'd seen. She woke Dick up and said, "Dick, I want to buy that house! I am

The house of Darrington Lane

lusting for it." Dick said, "Oh, Sal, go to sleep. We'll call Forrie in the morning." Sally says it was "the easiest sale Forrie ever made." Sally felt such a splurge was possible because she had just sold the place at Steamboat Springs. Since the marketers at Shalimar wanted to continue showing the model for the remainder of the year, Dick and Sally would not take possession until the following fall. The new house would be Sally's wedding gift to Dick.

Sally enjoyed shopping much more than Dick did, so he would often wait in the car with his newspaper and the radio until she returned. This day she was shopping for furniture for the new house, and after she'd been gone quite a while, she climbed back into the car as Dick said in his perfect droll deadpan, "I was beginning to think it was a hostage situation."

In the meantime Dick and Sally purchased seasons' tickets to Disney World and Epcot that were made available to residents of Florida at a special reduced price. They loved going at 3:00 in the afternoon to listen to "The American Singers" and watch the French mime. Sometimes they might stay for the parade or check out something that was new. Then they would enjoy dinner at one of the many international restaurants where authentically prepared ethnic dishes were served.

They purchased tickets for the season at two theaters where they enjoyed productions each month with different friends after enjoying dinner together. Every Monday night they played duplicate bridge. Dick was a good bridge player, not a master like Ward, but a good player. He and Sally made a competitive team who won many tournaments. Rather than belonging to a regular weekly bridge group, Sally preferred to fill in at various bridge games when she was needed because she was involved in so many other activities, one of which was teaching bridge classes.

Dick and Sally were avid participants in the Polk County Senior Games. Their friend Jim Berry was an organizer of the games. Dick earned 25 gold medals as "Best in His Age" at various activities, particularly fly casting for accuracy and distance, landing it closest to target. Fly-casting was a passion he had long shared with his brother Jack. Watching them was like watching a symphony in motion. However, one year Dick was quite dismayed to see a tiny young woman in her 50s wearing sandals step up and cast a line with perfect accuracy further than he had. He continued to hold the record for "Best in Age Group," but he was driven to beat her too. She kept him practicing.

A number of the friends Dick and Sally knew in high school who had places at Forest Lake also chose to winter at Shalimar in Florida..

Time for golf

They formed the nucleus of a social group in both places that attracted new friends who regularly did things together.

Dick and Sally hosted the Forest Lake Open in Florida for many years. If you won it, you got to host it the next year. It drew about 30 participants for golf, but it also offered alternate activities for those who didn't play. The Open drew attendees from many places in Michigan, not just Forest Lake.

At Shalimar someone, often Sally, would dream up some great rationale for a party. Their first party was for Sam's graduation from obedience school. Sally found a mortarboard and a blue cape for Sam to wear. They laughed together over the memory of Sam's very first lesson at obedience school. Sam and Dick were at the first station where Sam was to practice his first skill. Sam spotted all the other dogs that were there– perhaps five leaders working with ten dogs each. Sam promptly lifted his leg and "marked" Dick's leg to notify all those other dogs, "Don't get any ideas. He's mine."

Sam's graduation

Looking down, Dick was surprised at the warm stream against his leg and muttered in an embarrassed and mildly scolding tone, "Sam!?!" A trainer leaned over to Dick and said, "I've heard of that, but this is the first time I've seen it." Sally who was watching from the bleachers was beside herself with laughter.

Sally had been talking with Dick about what they would feed people at the graduation party, and Dick said, "Oh, no. I've got that covered. We'll have lasagna." He promptly went out and purchased pre-prepared Stouffer's frozen lasagna. Sally was a little taken aback. With the exception of an occasional purchase of prepared pizza dough, Sally always made everything from scratch. But the lasagna looked and smelled great, and all she did was add a salad. The Booths made a cake out of dog biscuits, and everyone brought doggie presents as well. It was a great party at which Sam felt quite pleased.

The crew was made up primarily of the Pingles, the Berries, the Wagners and the Snyders, though sometimes it might expand to 24. Sally had downsized when she'd married Dick and no longer had the banquet sized quantity of silverware and dishes she had always had. She scouted Goodwill but ended up buying a whole new set to have enough matching pieces.

They got together for all sorts of reasons and celebrated holidays like Thanksgiving or Easter together if they were away from their families. The hosting couple would prepare the main meat, and everyone would bring a dish. Marlene Pingle always brought her famous pecan pie and if Forrie Knapp came, he always brought shrimp. New Years Eve they would catch a movie after dinner at Fish City for dinner and then get together to watch the ball drop. New Years Day they often gathered to watch football and have chili at the Snyders'.

One memorable year Sally had prepared a full crockpot of chili for the crew on New Years Day and left it on warm while they went out for New Years Eve. When they got home, the empty crockpot was on the floor with nary a sign of the chili or the lid of the crockpot. They looked at their satisfied-looking and mildly guilty looking dog and realized he must have eaten not only the chili, but the glass lid as well. Alarmed, Sally called the vet, prepared for some kind of emergency procedure. The vet laughed and reassured her that the lid was tempered glass without sharp edges and that the dog would naturally "pass" it without any problem. He did. In the meantime, Sally went to her Plan B for serving her guests.

Each year when winter had finally ended in the north, it was time for the friends to leave Florida. The time of year was marked by a series of "must go meal" get-togethers. One couple would empty the excess from their refrigerators, freezers and pantries and prepare it all as a meal and invite everyone to come. Then another and another would do the same until all their kitchens were trimmed down for departure. It was a great way to wind down the Florida season.

76 - Reston For a Quick Visit and Closure

Sally went to Reston, Virginia to visit her friend Pat Scott and to check in with the owner of the business she had established there and then sold. The new owner was somewhat behind in his payments. In speaking with him Sally learned that he too had been the victim of a scam perpetrated by another ruthless person in that same Virginia community. Sally felt a bit of satisfaction at last that when the owner took that person to court, the person was sent to jail.

In lieu of the money she was owed, they came to an agreement - he would order wicker furniture for Sally's new screened in porch in Florida.

The wicker furniture

77 - Dick's Wedding Gift

Dick's wedding gift to Sally was an addition to his bachelor pad at Forest Lake that would give Sally an airy kitchen open to a spacious family room with soaring windows that looked into the forest. Dick had arranged for a builder he trusted who also happened to raise goats to do the renovation while Dick and Sally were in Florida. Sally was delighted with the addition. With the lovely space to entertain, she was eager to add bridge to the growing list of activities she was busily incorporating into her new life with Dick at Forest Lake.

78 - Japan

They'd been married three years when they planned a trip to Japan, a first visit for Sally and a place of many memories for Dick. He had graduated in Civil Engineering from the University of Michigan and was sent there with the Navy, which was restoring the country's infrastructure so decimated by the atomic blasts.

In advance of their two-week trip, Dick had written to arrange a visit to the base where he had been stationed for two years. They received the necessary clearance. The day of their visit was 9/11/2002, a year after the attack on the World Trade Center. The base was closed except for essential personnel that day. They arrived by taxi and were surprised to be greeted at the gate as if long-awaited dignitaries and treated with the utmost respect. A vehicle with a driver/guide was waiting at their disposal They were escorted without question to any and every place they wished to go, including golf and lunch. Sally said, "I felt as if I was married to the admiral," while Dick maintained that his role had been of some significance though not really noteworthy.

Other than their day at the base, they traveled as members of a tour group of twelve and were "the mom and pop" of the much younger group. Everyone was limited to one bag a piece, and each person handled his or her own luggage. A young photographer insisted Sally trade bags with him, so Sally carried his much lighter bag with camera equipment while he carried her considerably heavier one. She loved the "bullet trains," the high speed, efficient transit with its cadre of ladies dressed in pink who kept the stations spotless at all times. Sally also enjoyed the spotlessly clean taxis with starched linen covers on the headrests and fresh flowers in the cup holders. When the driver got out to remove their bags from the trunk, Sally spotted his supply of fresh replacement linen. She noted a man who was impeccably and formally dressed, including a homburg hat, who stooped down and picked up a cigarette butt and deposited it in a trash container.

Sally was struck not only by how clean everything was but also by how polite and welcoming the people were. Little girls on a train offered Sally some of their candy. Other older schoolgirls were wearing knee socks at precisely the same height but not the natural, full

227

extension of the sock. When Sally asked why this was, they explained that the height of their socks was an indicator of their level in school. Sock glue was sold to keep each schoolgirl's socks at the correct level. Sally found the concept fascinating and bought some sock glue.

At the food markets, each perfect peach sat atop a lace doily, and each apple was polished and placed just so. The yolks of the eggs, to Sally's surprise, were bright orange. They visited a fish market early in the morning where freshly caught, still-flopping fish were laid out and buyers were bidding on them. Sally was amazed that there was no fishy smell at all. On stools at sushi bars people sat to select which wriggling sea creature before them would be killed and prepared before them to eat. She loved the foods prepared on the hibachi and the delights of the teahouses.

The traditional Japanese way of sleeping, on mats on the floor, sounded awfully uncomfortable to Sally, but she found she "slept like a baby" on them. The underlying tatami mat had a rice straw base and woven rush grass cover. Over it was placed other soft bedding and a long "fur" pillow. The entire bed could be rolled up and stored away.

They saw and drank in the culture, history and character of many cities, tasting new flavors and exploring new perspectives. Sally says, "It was a lovely trip." They returned tired but glowing.

79 - Creating a Bridge Club

Since she hadn't succeeded in finding a readymade group of bridge players at Forest Lake, in 2002 she took matters into her own hands, determined to create one. She asked around and followed leads and cobbled together a diverse group of eight women, some of whom were familiar with the game and some who weren't but were willing to learn. She clearly knew what she wanted everyone to know – the fundamentals, the rules, the strategies and the insights that had made the game such a joy for her. I was one of the eight.

This is how I came to know Sally. She organized lessons and then we practiced. She stoked us with information and then threw us into the pool where we did a lot of floundering while she threw us lifelines when we grew desperate. We all quickly added the sentence starter, "Sally says…" to our conversations.

When we seemed fairly ready, she laid out her vision. We would meet once a week at each other's houses, alternating the role of hostess. We would begin the day with little muffins and coffee at 8:00 and play, with beverages and snacks available, until lunch time. After the hostess provided lunch, we would play until mid-afternoon and break for dessert before playing on until 5:00. "Oh it's going to be so much fun!" she bubbled with such authentic glee that everyone just smiled back. She said, "I'll go first." She went on and modeled the hostessing protocol, perfectly executing exactly what she had proposed we all do.

In the beginning we stretched so hard to remember and apply what she'd taught us about the rules of bridge that by the time 5:00 o'clock came, we were brain dead, but the day's hostess was two steps beyond that. I remember feeling shell-shocked when five o'clock

Forest Lake Bridge Group
L to r, Del, Sally, Jean Kaeding, Terri Father, Judy Kelly, Margaret Hessler, Bonnie Knapp and Trudy Johnson

came, incapable of any more thoughts or words. Only gentle, soothing, wordless melodies, please. But slowly we gained stamina and became a real bridge club.

We all rose to the rigorous demands of hosting, while enjoying the weeks when it wasn't our turn. One day, after listening to some of us bemoaning the trials of being hostess, Sally proposed a change. She dubbed her proposed change, "Stone Salad" and told us the old European fable of "Stone Soup."

In it a clever but hungry traveler came to a village. He found a large pot, filled it with water from the stream, and put it over the community fire to boil. He explained to the poor villagers that he would put a particular stone in the water, and after it had cooked long enough, the villagers would all be invited to enjoy the wonderful soup in the pot. One villager, seeing nothing but a pot of water but believing the traveler's promise, thought he could make the soup even better and brought some carrots from his garden that he added to the pot. Seeing this, another villager brought onions, and still another brought a beef bone, and someone else a few potatoes and so on until the village began to smell the savory soup that now filled the pot and soon filled the bellies of the hungry traveler as well as the community.

So in our bridge club, the hostess now provided the greens and dressings, while everyone brought whatever they wished to add to our "Stone Salad" – cucumbers, tomatoes, onions, nuts, beets, croutons, eggs, berries. Each week it was different and easy and delicious, lightening a great deal the work of the hostess..

In 2014 the bridge group gathered over lunch to honor Sally with these words:

We are going to take this moment, Sally, to remind you of how much we appreciate the happy impact you've made on our lives in this little spot in mid-Michigan.

It was your vision of a bridge group about 12 years ago that drew us out of our separate niches.

It was your skill and determination that challenged and encouraged us.

It was your optimistic patience that waited as many of us finally began to figure things out for ourselves.

And it was your delight in food and conversation that made us more than just folks playing bridge.

Out of it all we've become friends who trust, listen, lament and celebrate the events of each other's lives.

80 - Ah, Sweet Blackjack

Sally and Dick were great supporters of Casino Night at Forest Lake. They made themselves available to run tables as dealers and dressed the parts.

Sally also organized blackjack classes at the lake to pass on the skills, insights and disciplines she had acquired. She explained that blackjack is the only casino gambling game in which a player actually has a 50% chance of winning, so it's possible to come out ahead. But to do so, one must play intelligently, knowing the facts, the rules, the odds and following a disciplined plan.

In the real world, she went on, getting back 20% on an investment is considered a great success. So people who go in expecting to make back 50% or more are destined to be disappointed almost always.

Instead, to come out ahead in the long run, it's essential to have a plan for "how to lose." She says you can have the fun of playing all day without falling below the amount you came in with. When you make your goal, she says, you get up and leave. If you hit a lucky streak, you play until you lose three times in a row, and then you get up and leave.

At a casino, each table is posted with a required minimum bet. It could be $1.00 or $5.00 or $25.00 or $400.00 or... Sally uses a system for progressive bidding. She usually starts at a $5.00 table and bets twice the table limit. If she loses she puts out another $10.00. Her loss ceiling is always 30 X the table's minimum bet. If she reaches that, she moves on and tries again somewhere else. But if she wins, she pays herself back and then is playing with "the house money," not her own. When there are combinations that come up when the dice are rolled, there are some you bet on and some you don't depending on the odds that apply to each. There is much for the player to know and consider.

Sally's six-week classes drew many guys. Most were not interested in becoming knowledgable or disciplined but were in a hot hurry to play. Sally held out as a carrot the actual playing of the game until they could demonstrate they had learned the necessary essentials to be good players. Then she often watched as they threw it all aside to respond to an impulse or a hunch when they looked at the cards they were dealt.

When she and Ward lived in a community with a nearby casino, she might find a cute note from Ward on the fridge saying, "We need a little money for groceries. Let's go gambling this weekend." Ward supported his wife's love of blackjack because she played so skillfully and almost always came home with more than she'd arrived with. The week before a trip to the casino Ward would deal for Sally as she "counted cards," which is the mental discipline of keeping a running count in one's head of all the cards as they are played. She would arrange for a babysitter and explain to the kids, "Mama's going to work."

Counting cards uses a simplified counting system in which ten through ace are negative one. Two through six are plus one, and seven, eight, and nine are neutral. The system allows the skillful player to complete on a more even playing field with the otherwise superior odds of the "house."

Card counting is not illegal, but casinos are on the lookout for those who practice it because it cuts into their profits. So after noticing Sally was consistently successful over long periods, the dealer would start reshuffling after every deal. Unfortunately that cut into their grocery money. Still, Sally was rather flattered as a young mother with many children and little money to be seen as a threat as a "card counter."

81 - The Unresolved Tension With Ed

Ten years after Dick and Sally married, she was still bothered by the unresolved tension with Ed, her only sibling. She, Dick, Ehren and Becky decided to make a trip to the property he'd inherited from Minnie in northern Michigan and get things back on a more even footing. Ehren plotted out the route, and the four, bearing gifts of food, arrived without difficulty. They were surprised to see that the wooded 80 acres they called Meyer Camp had been logged. They would learn that Ed had sold a company the right to clear the land, something Minnie had never wanted to happen, but Ed needed the money.

Ed was there with his son John and dog Chester, but they were living in horrible conditions. The cabin, their clothes and their bodies were unwashed, and they seemed to be subsisting on cans of Dinty Moore beef stew, boxes of macaroni and cheese and food delivered by Meals On Wheels.

After a friendly but awkward visit, the four got back in the car to return to Forest Lake. They were all quiet, devastated by what they had found and unsure as to how to begin to right the situation. They decided the best thing to do was to call Ed's eldest daughter Mary Ellen, the doctor in Bariboo, Wisconsin. Mary Ellen hurried to the cabin and took control of the situation. She found a motel where her father and brother could bathe. She disposed of their clothes and found fresh ones at the Good Will. She took them to the barbershop, got them a good meal, and headed back with them to Bariboo where she situated her dad in the assisted living facility she operated. She saw to it that John was placed in a group home that could meet his needs.

Kristy and Mary Ellen had remained in touch over the years, and once Ed and John were stable in Baraboo, the cousins arranged another meeting between Ed and Sally. This time Kristy accompanied Sally on the pilgrimage. Ed was having difficulty with one leg and using a wheelchair, but the siblings were able to at last reach a level of peace and reconciliation. They had always loved each other and again acknowledged it, late though it was.

Then one day several years later Ed announced without drama to those in the assisted living facility where he lived, "I will die today," and he did.

It was one of the myriad premonitions and astonishing unexplainable events that have occurred in the line that flows through Minnie and her progeny.

His daughter Joanna remembered her dad:

Ed Meyer

"A man who played on the ground with his giggling children,
Who stopped the car on a back road and blasted "Jeremiah Was a Bullfrog" on the radio so the whole family could dance in the road,
Who created a successful restaurant business despite significant dyslexia and impulsivity,
Who scared the hiccups out of us with a great roar,
Who patiently taught us to hunt, fish, play cards and prepare food in the most delicious ways,
Who taught us by example to appreciate nature, trust people, forgive easily take life lightly and follow your passions.

82 - Sugar Springs

Sally and Dick were quite content splitting their busy lives between Florida and Forest Lake. For twenty years they piled Tiger and Sam and then Tucker after Sam died into the car to make the trip to and then back from Florida. They refined a system for the motels they stopped at en route. Sally would stay in the car as Dick registered, saying that he had a dog. He always requested a room near a corridor exit where he could take Sam or Tucker out do their business. Then parking near that door and with it open, Sally would whisk Tiger in his crate into the room and put it in the bathtub. After leaving him with his dinner and his litter box in the bathroom, they would take Sam with them for dinner and then return for the night. After Sam died and they got Tucker, they continued the same procedure. There was, however, one difference – Tucker, not Tiger was the alpha male.. Tiger held his own, but he clearly was no longer in charge.

Sally decided that continuing to own the little house just across Willow Street on Davies Place in Denver that she had inherited from Minnie didn't make sense anymore. She was advised that if she was going to sell the house, a way to avoid the $25,000 capital gains tax would be to buy another more expensive property and rent it for two years. They were in no hurry to leave their charming place at Forest Lake, but $25,000 was $25,000. They shopped and found a lovely home on the water at Sugar Springs about 40 minutes from Forest Lake It was a community of upscale second homes for people who lived and worked elsewhere in the state. As the CPA advised, they rented it for two years

Sugar Springs house

and continued happily living at Forest Lake. Then it was time to implement the rest of the plan. They would sell the Forest Lake house and move to Sugar Springs since they couldn't pay for and maintain three houses. It was a painful move for them and for their many friends at Forest Lake. But though they made new friends and found new activities at Sugar Springs, they continued their longtime involvement at Forest Lake.

Now, since they were living directly on a lake, Dick sent for plans for a boat that he would construct in the garage. He worked diligently and happily on it, and when it was finished, invited their friends for the christening and launch.

The boat that Dick built

The men, laughing in their summer shorts, trekked the boat from the garage and after christening it, launched it beside the dock where it promptly sank to the amazement and uproarious laughter of the friends. They hoisted it back out of the water, Dick saying it appeared there was a little more work he needed to do on it. They celebrated anyway, and the next day Dick was easily able to find the spot he had neglected to caulk to make it seaworthy.

After several well-spent years, they put the Sugar Springs house on the market, but timing was terrible. The economy was descending into recession, and the houses that were snapped up like hotcakes when Dick and Sally bought at Sugar Springs were now remaining on the market despite deeper and deeper price cuts. There were no buyers. Finally, despite having to face a loss of $40,000, they accepted an offer and moved on, downsizing in the process.

83 - Plan B: The Little House

They had a plan B. When Dick initially bought property at Forest Lake, he purchased over half the block of lots between Bobwhite and Roughed Grouse.

Dick's daughter Ehren met Becky Deshone when they were both respiration therapists in the same hospital. A wonderful, warm relationship blossomed, and the two married several years later. Dick proudly walking both brides down the "aisle" at the beautiful gardens of Edgewood Golf Course which was owned by friends.

Sally, Becky, Ehren, Dick

So having sold both of their northern houses, Dick and Sally designed a small house that would nestle snugly into the trees on another of Dick's lots at Forest Lake close to Ehren and Becky's house. It would have one large, flexible, studio room with a full kitchen that ran all along the back plus a bathroom and a sweet front porch that looked out over what would become a lovely garden. A Murphy bed tucked itself away cleverly into a wall of bookcases and drawers for storage, allowing floor space for larger gatherings. There was a desk for Dick, an expandable table and flexibly usable furniture. Dick created paintings of Sally's beloved red geraniums for the walls.

Little House at Forest Lake

Sally's favorite, geraniums painted by Dick

     The little house would be the home base for Dick and Sally when they came back from Florida for summers. Ultimately it would become Ehren and Becky's. Dick had put up a good portion of the money for the materials and construction of the house as a part of Ehren's inheritance. Becky and Ehren had put up the rest.

     Dick and Sally settled easily into the little house, built by the same contractor who had built Dick's original house at Forest Lake. They resumed their active and multifaceted life in the north, working around health issues when they cropped up.

84 - Dick Becomes Ill

Then in 2018, the year they would both turn 89, a health issue got the best of Dick. Everyone, including Dick and Sally, did what they could to reverse its inroads, but this time things declined beyond return. The thought of losing Dick was devastating, but the thought of his lingering on endlessly without quality of life was even worse. After several weeks he slipped away, but not without a parting gift. He had been comatose for days when a nurse bent over him and said, "Mr. Snyder, are you comfortable?" In classic droll Dick Snyder form he replied, "I make a living." The vigil continued as his light flickered dimmer and dimmer. Sally had left his bedside for a few brief break when Dick seemed to breathe his last. Ehren called Sally on her cell, telling her, "Dad's stopped breathing." Ehren turned to her dad and said, 'Hold on, Dad, she's on her way." And he somehow did -long enough for Sally to race to his side and lift his hand to hold it one last time. "Good night, sweet prince," Ehren said for all who so deeply loved him.

The memorial service was held at the clubhouse at Forest Lake on his 89th birthday, May 5, 2018. The first words in the program were by Helen Lowrie Marshall, and they set the tone for the afternoon.

I'd like the memory of me to be a happy one.
I'd like to leave an afterglow of smiles when life is done.
I'd like to leave an echo whispering softly down the ways,
Of happy times and laughing times and bright and sunny days.
I'd like the tears of those who grieve to dry before the sun
Of happy memories that I leave when life is done.

Reverend Mike who had presided at the wedding of Ehren and Becky conducted the service with wonderful grace. It was a tear-filled but joyous celebration of Dick Snyder and his life. There was Nat King Cole's recording of "Smile," a favorite of Dick's that was written by another favorite of his, Charlie Chaplin. Dick's brother Jack, Ehren, Sally and friends shared poignant and often funny memories of their times with Dick.

Sally concluded with:

"May you all experience the complete understanding and love that communicates by holding hands in private. It's just so right.

Thank you, Dick."

We listened to the beautiful, soaring Nessun Dorma from Puccini's opera, "Turandot," another of Dick's favorites. Then after the closing prayer came the strains of "The Victors," the fight song of Dick's beloved University of Michigan Wolverines.

2018...
Each New Now

85 - A New Chapter

There was nothing for Sally to do but keep moving as she always had; her first question, "What are the givens and what shall I do with them?"

She returned to their winter home in Florida where their friends embraced her as they all missed Dick together - the now missing piece in a lovely set. She also made the practical decision to put the house on the market. While awaiting a buyer, she would rent it when she could, or come to stay in it when it was not rented.

She would again shift her base of operations back to Denver and to the house on Willow Street she had built 60 years earlier when her nomadic military family was ready for a permanent place to call home. It had for years been Pam and David's home, and they had welcomed Sally back to join them.

While Pam continued working at Craig Hospital providing hope and pathways forward for people confronting life-changing trauma or

| Sally and Pam in conversation | The ambiance of the Willow Street Home |

catastrophic loss, Pam worked to make the Willow Street home a refuge and comfort for the three of them. Pam made the gardens of the backyard her canvas, painted with growing things and colorful birds, and Sally drank in their healing beauty and diversity each day. Sally and Pam both loved cooking and baking, and together they took delight in making the most of each season's bounty.

Karen quilting

Nearby was Karen who had pursued an active career as a teacher of children, a teacher of teachers, and an administrator in the schools of both Alaska and Arizona.When her husband Lewis died, she'd returned to Denver to find her center again.

She found and decorated an airy condo in which she designated a studio space for creating the magnificent quilts that emerge from her inspired fingers. Together she and Sally could take advantage of opportunities to "fondle fabric." Karen observed that it seemed remarkable that whatever her age, her mother always seemed to be that same age too.

Colorado Springs where David and his wife Dale lived was only an hour or so south of Denver. The historic old home they had restored bustled with energy, hospitality, creativity, and with delicious things to eat. David worked in his "Art Box" studio in the backyard where he channeled his talents through photography and art. Sally felt wonderfully at home in the midst of her son's dynamically inventive life.

Sally and David

Sally flew to Cape Cod and spent busy, laid back, creative, fulfilling weeks with Kris, her husband James, their

245

sweet family, and dog, Tess. Kris had retired from a career in the schools where she was a well-revered leader in the field of occupational therapy.

When Sally and Kris were together, they automatically gathered thought-provoking ideas and generated hands-on projects that they couldn't wait to undertake. All of these they shared long distance with Karen and Pam who, like them, loved having their hands busy and minds stimulated.

One notion that they pondered came from Naomi Shihab Ny's poem that ended:

"I want to be famous in the way a pulley is famous,
Or a buttonhole, not because it did anything spectacular,
But because it never forgot what it
could do."

When one of Sally's daughter or Ehren or Becky found a book she really enjoyed, she would invite the others to read it too so that they could discuss it.They all especially adored books by Louise Penny *(introduced to them by Ehren)* and were drawn to her *Four Statements That Lead to Wisdom:*

I'm sorry
I don't know
I need help
I was wrong

Now the readers are planning a Louise Penny trip to rural Quebec near the Vermont border to see for themselves the locale that inspired her stories.

Never idle, Sally often carries with her for long stays the yarn and small knitting needles she employs to knit the stunning, small, three-dimensional, intricate, multi-charactered, multi-creatured nativity tableau that she plans to donate as a fundraiser for a worthy cause.

The loss of beautiful Ralph, the kind, perceptive, talented, generous, youngest Beightol was almost too much to bear. Despite his dyslexia, he'd completed his college degree, married, and pursued a highly successful career in business. He designed and built a magnificent home. But beneath the surface, the combination of his dyslexia and his inherited susceptibility to alcoholism increasingly took their toll. He would seem to be fine until suddenly he was not fine at all. Then he would rehabilitate and recover, and everyone would hope again until… Still, no one was prepared for the excruciating loss of Ralph and the gaping hole it left in the family.

Ralph

86 - Hawaii

The family delighted Sally on her 90th birthday with the announcement that she and her kids would celebrate the great event together the following year with a gala trip to Hawaii the month of her 91st birthday. So in April of 2020 David, Dale, Kris, James, Karen, Pam and Sally flew to the exquisite, tropical island of Kauai in the mid Pacific to celebrate the irrepressible matriarch of a clan Kris called a

Sally and Kris in Hawaii for Sally's 91st Birthday

"family of sweethearts." It was a wonderful celebration which concluded perfectly just before the covid19 virus descended like a cloud over the world.

As Sally says, "We really did it!" They stayed at a lovely place looking directly out over the turquoise ocean. She was introduced to Mai Tais and laughed at the surprising presence of feral chickens everywhere. Years before, storms had pummeled the islands and freed the chickens kept by farmers in coops and pens. Delighted with their freedom, they've been happily procreating ever since.

Every day was an adventure, Sally said, and every night they splurged, enjoying leisurely and delicious meals at the very best restaurants. One day they took an amazing helicopter tour along the dramatic Nepali coast and over the remarkable geologic formations of the island. The flight was far more comprehensive than they had expected because the owner of the helicopter had invited along several personal friends whom he really wanted to impress. One day they took a train through a diverse plantation where they had tastings of what was produced there. They were indulged with a festive luau, and then the night before they left, the family gifted Sally with a book of appreciations they had created for the mom they so deeply adored.

It was in the form of a time capsule that held maybe a dozen letters from members of the family. They cited traditions that Sally had started and special things that Sally had created like the girls' "sissy" and "piggy" dresses and" the memorable "Alice in Wonderland Party." They noted Sally's way of looking at things: "How did they do that?" And figuring out, "I can do that."

There was the way she started a talk with something fun or attention getting that allowed people to relax and pay attention. There was her explanation to David that changed his way of looking at life after someone at school bullied him about the green socks he was wearing. There was her good business sense, resilience and creative leadership reflected in the refrain, "Who......? Sally, by golly."

87 - Yes to the New Day

Observant Sally in her nineties enters each new day open to what it may hold and ready to figure out what she may add to it. "Oh look… snow on the peaks this morning." "Oh look… chickadees at the feeder. Oh, this coffee smells wonderful. Pam, 'll bake a pie with those peaches in the refrigerator. We can have it with Sarah and the kids this afternoon. I see there's a message on my cell phone that the apples on our neighbor's tree are all ripe. They're going to bring them Thursday with sugar, and we'll make applesauce. That'll be great! There's one from Karen about the new exhibit at the museum. I'll tell her we'll go Wednesday because Thursday we're busy."

It's not that the beloved body that allows her spirit to operate in the world can always keep pace with her drive. It frequently complains to Sally; sometimes rebels and even downright refuses, insisting that it "can't." But Sally cajoles and insists that, " Yes, it can!" And once she has it up and the motor running, the two are on their way.

Laughter spills easily from her lips as do tears when her eyes when her heart is touched. She adores geraniums, children, dogs, poems, songs, stories, adventures, culinary, bridge, blackjack and he delicious and beautiful wherever she finds it. She is a woman of faith who prays and then moves her feet.

The Willow Street house is a light-filled respite where both new beginnings and years of memories are nurtured. The window to the mountains invites reflection on the wonder of each day. The door opposite it goes to the garden filled with birds - where roots are quietly unfurling the energy of buds and blossoms. The door to the garden is one Sally found in an antique store.

 She loved it because its etched glass window reminded her of the Red Cedar River that ran
through the campus of Michigan State where her life with Ward Beightol began its great adventure.

The house became Pam's in 1998 when Sally and Dick married, but it still enfolds the Beightol children who grew to adulthood in it. And now it embraces their children as well as their own grandchildren.

Central to the house is the expandable dining table where for decades meals and stories have been shared, games played, projects executed, ideas verbalized and comfort given. It even exists as an archive of the special guests who have dined with the family and who have been invited to sign their names and the dates of their visits on the underside of its leaves.

And it is where Sally and I pored over pictures and documents as we visited moments of Sally's life to gather the elements of this book.

"The Table"

The table and door to the verdant backyard

88 - Seeming More Than Coincidence

Some events seem to be more than mere coincidence when they serve to so clearly unite the past with the present and future. When granddaughter Kate was a student completing a course in Paris several years after Ward died, her mom Kris and grandma Sally flew to join her. The three went to Notre Dame where they were immersing themselves in its history and beauty when sound suddenly flooded over them that took their breath away. Out of nowhere stepped an American boys choir singing "Amazing Grace," Ward's signature song, in barbershop harmony. The three generations were overwhelmed with the assurance that Ward had found them in his beloved Paris and had pulled some strings to be able to join them and shower his greeting on them.

Then in 1998 Pam received a postcard at the Willow Street house from an author, Robert Callahan, who was promoting his book, On Wings of Troop Carriers. Pam saw that it included pictures and narrative of times that her dad would have been on active duty during World War II, so she ordered the book. It came with a note of appreciation from the author, and Pam wrote back explaining about when and where her dad had served and mentioning that she had a few items of his from the war. He responded, explaining that a group was establishing a museum along the French and Belgian border that would commemorate the heroic efforts made by Americans to liberate that region from the Nazis during World War II. He was interested in what she might have. But then after another exchange, Pam decided that what she had was similar to what the museum had already collected, so she put the letter aside.

Then when recently Pam went to California to help her daughter Sarah and her family move back to Colorado, she came upon a large leather briefcase. She asked Sarah about it, but Sarah realized she didn't know anything about it. All she could think was that it must have inadvertently been moved along with her things.

When they sat down to open the briefcase, they discovered it contained a collection of items Ward had saved. Most dated from the years he was on active duty in Europe during World War II. There were letters from military friends talking about what they were doing at the various stations they were posted. There were flight plans and maps of terrain in Europe where they were flying. There were his navigation instruments. One letter was from Arnie Anderson, Ward's great friend from their time together in Paris during the war - the same fellow for whom Ward had denied his interest in Sally at Michigan State because he thought she was Arnie's girlfriend.

Sally and Karen in Alaska

Some of these may well be of interest to the museum Robert Calhoun had spoken of, Pam and Sarah agreed. So Pam and Sally are now considering personally delivering Ward's briefcase to the museum if they find that the museum exists and would want their items.

A convenience that would facilitate such a trip for Sally in her nineties is the international time-share that Sally bought when Ward retired from the military. She bought it when she realized that after Ward retired, he and Sally could fly standby free of charge to anyplace in the world. Sally saw the beauty of having the time-share to arrange accommodations in advance for the places they would visit. But Ward and Sally could not make use of the perk before Ward died, and the flight perk ended with his death.

Sally retained the time-share and was able to use it for special wedding gifts, and the family used it for various trips and special occasions. Shortly after Dick and Sally were married, they used it for a wonderful cruise to Alaska where they visited with Karen who was working there as superintendent of schools.

When they returned from that trip, Dick reasoned that since they already had two vacation homes, they really did not

Sally on the Alaska cruise

need the time-share. At that point Kris and James decided to take over the time share, and it now continues to be a boon to the whole active family. In lieu of buying gifts for each other for Christmas, the Beightol clan comes together at least once a year in various places. One year the time share was used for a yacht in Boston Harbor for the 4th of July and another time for the yacht at New Years. The family has visited the mountains using the time-share and then Kauai for the celebration of Sally's 90th birthday when she was 91.

And now Sally and Pam are pondering an adventure using the time share for a trip taking Ward's things to the museum in Europe where they will be honored and preserved as a part in history..

Grass does not grow under the feet of Sally or her family.

89 - The Soup

Sally is a wonderful cook, the daughter, granddaughter and daughter-in-law of wonderful cooks. She is in the kitchen what she has always been in life - the creator of nutritious and tasty things from whatever ingredients she finds about her. She loves food as she loves life and people, and she's passed on those loves to her family. Good food and good company matter.

Years ago she found a wooden drawer from a library's card catalog in an antique shop. It now holds nearly a yard of her recipes -- some from her Grandma Flora, some from her mom, some from Ward's mom, and hundreds she's created or gathered herself.

But there's one that originated in Ward's frugal but playful mind. Despite the Depression ravaging the country during her childhood, Sally grew up in a family where there was no shortage of food. Her father Fred was in the groceries business, and her mother Minnie canned fruits that grew in their yard. As a result, Sally was inclined to throw leftovers away.

You may recall that when Sally and Ward were newlyweds, Ward asked her about the peas that were left over from dinner the night before. When Sally admitted that she had thrown them out, Ward was dismayed. "Oh no, Sally," he shook his head, "We never waste food." Leftovers needed to be refrigerated or frozen until there was enough to make soup. After all, they still had good nutritional value.

So Sally ever after kept a jar in the refrigerator or freezer to which she added leftover peas, corn, peppers, beans, carrots and whatever until she had enough for soup. She made soup periodically, and the kids didn't consider it a big deal.

But when Ward came home from Greenland in the middle of his deployment, he told the kids he had brought them a surprise: the ingredients for "Penguin Soup." It sounded exotic and exciting, and given their expectations, they were delighted and found it remarkably tasty and delicious, even though it in reality contained no penguin. It was vegetable soup.

Now Penguin Soup is on the menu in the homes of all the Beightol children and even of their grandchildren. There is always a jar in the refrigerator or freezer to which one adds leftovers until there's enough for soup. Penguin Soup has become part of the family's culinary heritage. It smilingly reminds everyone to make use of even the small gifts of life and that when we *expect* to find delight, we are well on the way to *discovering* it. Good food for body and soul.

I asked Sally if there was an actual recipe for penguin soup. "Well, yes," she answered:

Penguin Soup

"Start with a good soup bone with as much
      meat left on it as possible.
Put it in a pot of water and bring it to a boil.
Add:
      1 head of cabbage,
      2 or 3 onions,
      1 can of tomato soup or tomato paste or sauce
Add the vegetables you've been saving.
Add salt to taste.
Last of all, throw
    a handful of peppercorns into the soup
Leave it to simmer all day.

You can then strain them out since their work is done, but you can also leave them in to suddenly surprise your senses like tiny fireworks with their crunch and pizazz."

90 - The Arc of History

Saturday morning
January 16, 2021
9:00 Mountain Time for Sally in Denver
11:00 Eastern Time for Del in Charleston

Sally's words began our conversation.

"My story really can't begin with me. It has to begin with my mother's complicated story."

Through the years that the tiny sprout, Sally, was developing into the mature force she's become, her mother Minnie was beside her, modeling hard-won wisdom she had gained in her own complex life.

Though Minnie received scarcely any formal education, Sally describes her as "sharp as a whip." She simply figured things out her own way. She demonstrated that if you just looked at and studied something, you could probably figure out how it worked and do it or make it yourself if you tried. And Sally tried and did.

Sally watched her mother forge ahead in spite of her fears, making it clear that it's pointless to deny what is. Just get on with it. Assess the givens and look for options and a plan that will allow you to move forward. To this day, Sally leaves little time for lamenting or blaming. Instead she searches out the next good step in the right direction.

Because Minnie had none of the normal experiences of childhood, she and Sally often inquired, played, investigated, and discovered, simply as children growing up together. And when Sally became a young mother herself, it felt right and natural for her to set aside *grownup* activities in order to share the spontaneous wonder of playing with and growing up along with her children.

Minnie with her fish at Meyer Camp

Sally's vibrant life, unfolded in these pages, has its foundation in the resilient courage, wisdom and love of her mother, Minnie. And now it surges on as a powerful legacy through Sally to her beloved children, to their children, and to theirs...

The Legacy Flowing On - 1982

Top center - Sally with Ward below to her right,
Frank Flint to her left and Minnie seated below them.

In the far left corner is Lewis Ligon just above wife Karen Beightol Ligon

In front of Karen is James Mawhinney holding baby Kate and beside him, his
wife Kris Beightol Mawhinney

Above Kris is Ralph Beightol and to Ralph's left is Carl Kempainen

On Frank Flint's left is John Arnoldy, first husband of Pam Beightol who is
seated in front of him holding their first child, Sarah

In front of Pam and Sarah are David Beightol and son Carson
Above David is his first wife Deana holding baby Cole

Sally Ann Meyer Beightol Snyder

Acknowledgments

I am grateful for the love and integrity of two fine men in my life, first my husband Ward Beightol and then my husband Dick Snyder. The philosophical clarity and financial security they brought to our marriages provided me the freedom to pursue my own pathways of discovery.

I know everyone has a story. That my dear friend Del offered her time and talent to tell my story has been such a gift. All through the second year of the pandemic, our Saturday morning interviews brought us laughter and tears. My story became her story to tell. Thanks, Del.

Thanks to my talented photographer son David Beightol for editing and improving the quality of the photos used in this book. They add a rich level of meaning to the accompanying words.

And very special thanks to my beloved grandson Eric Arnoldy who leaped in with all of his patience and amazing skills to bring our project to completion.

Del extends her heartfelt thanks to Jena Copley who patiently found solutions for technical issues in integrating the pictures and formatting the book; to Scott Dixon who came to our rescue; to Kathleen Johnson who gave me immensely helpful advice in editing; to my sister Valerie Browne and friend Jocelyn Chabot who edited for errors and gifted me with moral support. And my deepest thanks to Eric Arnoldy whose gracious assistance in the final stages of publication has been invaluable. And of course, my enormous thanks to Sally for sharing her story with me.

66821189R00149